POWER
WITNESSING

How to
Witness to
Different
Personalities

POWER
WITNESSING

David A. Farmer

REVIEW AND HERALD® PUBLISHING ASSOCIATION
HAGERSTOWN, MD 21740

The author assumes full responsibility for the accuracy of all
facts and quotations as cited in this book.

This book was
Edited by Gerald Wheeler
Copyedited by Jocelyn Fay and James Cavil
Designed by Bill Kirstein
Electronic makeup by Shirley Bolivar
Typeset: 11/15 Garamond Book

PRINTED IN U.S.A.

03 02 01 00 99   5 4 3 2 1

R & H Cataloging Service
Farmer, David Allen, 1954-
    Power witnessing.
        1. Witness bearing (Christianity).   2. Evangelistic work.   I. Title.
            248.5

ISBN 0-8280-1403-5

This book is
DEDICATED TO
My Lord and Saviour,
for without Him none of it would have been possible.

To all my friends, church members, and family who
allowed me to use their stories.

To Len McMillan for giving me permission
to use his research.

To Bill Wampler, Fred Rimer, and Bruce Hinckley,
three men who gave me an opportunity to work for
my Lord and Saviour.

And to my incredibly loving wife, Kathy,
for her love, patience, and trust in me that inspired me
to write this book.

CONTENTS

INTRODUCTION

FOR YEARS now I have discovered that whenever anyone mentions the words "witnessing" or "evangelizing,"
many either yawn or become extremely uncomfortable in
their seats. Over the years hundreds of books have gathered
dust on the shelves of our local Adventist Book Centers, and
our conferences have many different videos on the subject
just waiting for pastors and members to ask for them. I think
we sometimes forget that those God called to proclaim the
three angels' messages have to be a people found sharing
God's message on every street corner, using every means
God has given us. "'Go ye into all the world, and preach the
gospel to every creature.' While so great a work remains to
be done, shall not we, as Christ's followers, arouse to a
sense of our God-given responsibility, and be active in doing
our part?" (*Atlantic Union Gleaner,* Nov. 4, 1908).

As a church we must have public seminars, evangelistic
meetings, branch Sabbath schools, and small group studies.
But I believe that as individuals we must work within a
framework that fits our nature. In other words, within our
temperaments and personality. "We all need to study character and manner that we may know how to deal judiciously with different minds" (*Testimonies for the Church,*
vol. 4, p. 69).

Witnessing can be easy if we learn to do it with the God-
given talents and gifts we each have. I believe it is essential
that we understand that we have come to a time in our
earth's history that only by renewing our witnessing ideas

are we going to finish God's mission. It is nearly impossible for pastors to do all the witnessing for the church. They have to have the help of the congregation in order to reach every door and listening ear. Don't they have enough on their shoulders already just trying to feed their local flock?

I remember a time I received a call to pastor a new district. Just before my district opened, the conference president asked me if I would hold an evangelistic series in another small district. The first Sabbath I was there, I traveled with the local pastor to one of the churches in his district. As we journeyed, he asked me if I could give him five minutes to write his sermon for that day. So on that beautiful Sabbath morning, while driving, the pastor prepared his sermon for the Sabbath service. And yes, it sounded just like a thrown-together-in-five-minutes sermon. No wonder his district was small and dying.

The same dilemma applies to witnessing. Trying to throw together an effective witnessing program quickly is like a pastor expecting to have a great and powerful sermon after whipping up something Sabbath morning on the way to church. It just will not work, because it takes time, energy, and much prayer. How can anyone ever expect to have a dynamic witnessing program if they try to produce it in five minutes? *The precious graces of the Holy Spirit are not developed in a moment.* Courage, fortitude, meekness, faith, unwavering trust in God's power to save, are acquired by the experience of years. By a life of holy endeavor and firm adherence to the right the children of God are to seal their destiny" (*ibid.,* vol. 8, p. 314; italics supplied).

I feel one of the most spiritually invigorating experiences Christians can have is a dynamic witnessing program. One that works for them, fitting their temperament and personality. "We differ so widely in disposition, habits, education, that our ways of looking at things vary. We judge differently. Our understanding of truth, our ideas in regard to the conduct of life, are not in all respects the same. There are no two whose experience is alike in every particular. The trials of one are not the trials of another. The duties that one finds light, are to another most difficult and perplexing" (*Gospel Workers,* p. 473).

There is nothing like seeing someone come to Christ! Once you experience it, you never want to let it go. It's a super high! But we have to remember that just because one program works for some doesn't guarantee it will reach everyone else.

Today I find that many people have real phobias about witnessing. I believe this happens mainly because many try to witness in ways not suited for them. It is my personal conviction that unless we learn to witness within our personality, we will not lead as many to Jesus as we could have. The closer we get to the Second Coming, the more we need to learn to spread the gospel in ways that others can understand and accept. "Time is very short, and all that is to be done must be done quickly. The angels are holding the four winds, and Satan is taking advantage of everyone who is not fully established in the truth. Every soul is to be tested. Every defect in the character, unless it is overcome by the help of God's Spirit, will become a sure means of destruction. I feel as never before the necessity for our people to be energized by the spirit of the truth, for Satan's devices will ensnare every soul who has not made God his strength. The Lord has much work to be done; and if we do what He has appointed for us to do, He will work with our efforts" (*Testimonies for the Church,* vol. 5, p. 573).

One way to witness that I believe can work for almost anyone is to understand the temperament theory. The concept isn't perfect, but in my view it can be an extremely helpful tool in grasping human behavior. Although not everyone accepts it, if used in a right perspective it can be an excellent aid in understanding why people act the way they do.

Following the simple steps, guidelines, and principles you will find in this book will make witnessing much easier and give you greater success. I trust these pages will help you learn how better to understand that witnessing within your temperament can be fun, exciting, and encouraging. I hope they will motivate and inspire you to try witnessing all over again. To taste it again for the first time, as the Kellogg's ads urge us to do with their cereal. And above all, I pray that by the time you are through reading this volume, you will have developed a closer relationship with Jesus.

Chapter 1

Working Within Our Temperament

My WIFE is one of those types who like to plan everything. Not too long ago we purchased a new vehicle and received a free trip to Branson, Missouri. Before we ever leave on any trip, Kathy expects me to study a map and find the shortest and safest route. If I get lost or take the wrong turn, she always has the same question: "Did you look at the map before we left?" I'm the type who likes to read the map along the route, hoping I haven't missed my turn.

Well, wouldn't you know it, on our way to Branson I made a wrong turn in Memphis, Tennessee, and she asked the question I knew was coming. The truth is that I had studied the map, but I still managed to make a wrong turn. When we did make it to Branson, we drove straight to the comedy show we wanted to see before we even checked into our motel. Because of my little unplanned detour in Memphis and the fact that I had miscalculated the distance by an hour and a half (maps can be so confusing when you try to judge by an inch scale) we arrived much later than we had planned. Kathy was a little concerned that they would sell our tickets to someone else who could read a map better than I could.

We walked into the lobby and found a line (of course, isn't there always?) and had to wait until those ahead of us could choose their seats (some people have a harder time making up their mind than others do). It would take a good five to 10 minutes (so it seemed) for each couple to choose the best seats in the house suited for them. By the time we got up to the window, we were just hoping to be able to find two seats beside each other. But they still had our seats waiting for us—third row, end seats. Just exactly what my wife had asked for and reserved weeks earlier. Everything turned out perfectly! Why? Because my wife has a melancholy temperament.

Kathy had planned everything long before we ever left home. She prepared the menu for each day's meals, got reservations for the shows we were to see (something we sanguines would never think of), made sure we had enough cash, and asked if I had looked at the map to figure out the best route to take. You name it, she had planned it.

I, on the other hand, was just eager to get in the car and on the road with two or three hours behind us. Why should I look at a map? After all, I had traveled that way before, and besides, we got to see a lot of Memphis we had never visited before. When we finally arrived in Branson, I wanted to go to the motel first and freshen up before we purchased our tickets. They would keep them for us until we arrived, even if we were a little late. Why backtrack and travel to the same place twice?

Kathy almost never forgets anything. She will worry for the first couple hours after we start our trip, wondering if she has forgotten anything. Me, I almost always forget something. But so what if I occasionally leave behind my toothbrush, deodorant, pillow, belt, or tie? I can buy another one when I get there. That will give me a reason to check out the local K Mart. You never know what sort of blue-light special they might be having on something we need.

All and all, it was a great trip to Branson! With Kathy's quiet, analytical, and gifted spirit and my fun-loving, enthusiastic, and talkative nature we were able to have fun and do a lot more than we had planned to do at first. Her sensitive and emotional nature helped me to appreciate the finer art of music and professional musical talent. All I desired to hear was the country and western foot-stomping music and lots of jokes. She wanted to hear gospel music and see the dancing water show. Both of us love country and western gospel, just at different rhythms and tempos. What makes the difference between us? Our temperaments!

Our temperaments influence everything we do, from our sleeping habits to the way we eat and communicate with each other. Temperaments combine the traits that we inherited from our parents and make us what we are—outgoing and extrovert, shy and introvert, or anything else. They shape whether we like art, music, or sports.

Nothing is more powerful or has more influence in our lives than our temperaments. That is why I believe we should study not only our own temperament, but those of other people as well. Ellen White clearly points out that "we all need to study *character* and *manner* that we may know how to *deal judiciously* with different minds, that we may use our best endeavors to help them to a correct understanding of the Word of God and to a true Christian life. . . . The person must be shown his true character, *understand his own peculiarities* of disposition and temperament, and see his infirmities" (*Testimonies for the Church,* vol. 4, p. 69; italics supplied). "In order to lead souls to Jesus there must be a knowledge of human nature and a study of the human mind. Much careful thought and fervent prayer are *required to know how to approach* men and women upon the great subject of truth" (*ibid.,* p. 67; italics supplied).

Every witness for Christ needs to understand clearly how the human mind works in order to help others make a favorable decision for God. We can reach people for God better when we know what they are thinking, their convictions, and the desire of their hearts. Since our temperaments are who and what we are made up of, shouldn't we study to understand them better? "Mechanics, lawyers, merchants, men of all trades and professions, educate themselves that they may become masters of their business. Should the followers of Christ be less intelligent, and while professedly engaged in His service be ignorant of the ways and means to be employed?" *(ibid.).* Before we are able to do God's work, we must first understand the ones we are speaking to and discern what makes them tick.

Ellen White observes that "the life of John was not spent in idleness, in ascetic gloom, or in selfish isolation. From time to time *he went forth* to mingle with men; and he was ever an interested observer of what was passing in the world. From his quiet retreat he watched the unfolding of events. With vision illuminated by the divine Spirit *he studied the characters of men,* that he might understand how to reach their hearts with the message of heaven" (*The Desire of Ages,* p. 102; italics supplied). Elsewhere she adds: "The *secret of our success* and power as a people advocating advanced truth will be found in making direct, personal appeals to those who are interested, having unwavering reliance upon the Most High" (*Review and Herald,* Aug. 30, 1892; italics supplied).

Proverbs 11:30 declares that "the fruit of the righteous is a tree of life, and he who wins souls is wise" (NKJV). The great aim and mission of the church has always been to take the gospel into all the world. If you and I are not doing our part to help fulfill the mission God has laid out for His church, then we have no right to claim to be part of a church that professes to be the remnant.

"Christians will have the mind of Christ, and be coworkers with him. *To every one work has been allotted,* and no one else can be a substitute for another. *Each one has a mission* of wonderful importance, which he cannot neglect or ignore. . . . God has appointed His children to give light to others, and if they fail to do it, and souls are left in the darkness of error because of their failure to do that which they might have done, had they been vitalized by the Holy Spirit, they will be accountable to God" (*Review and Herald,* Dec. 12, 1893; italics supplied).

"He who seeks to give light to others will himself be blessed. 'There shall be showers of blessing.' 'He that watereth shall be watered also himself.' Prov. 11:25. God could have reached His object in saving sinners without our aid; but in order for us to develop a character like Christ's, we must share in His work. In order to enter into His joy—the joy of seeing souls redeemed by His sacrifice—we must participate in His labors for their redemption" (*The Desire of Ages,* p. 142).

"This is a responsibility from which we cannot free ourselves. *Our words, our acts, our dress, our deportment, even the expression of the countenance, has an influence"* (*Christ's Object Lessons,* p. 339; italics supplied).

Through the years I have become more and more convinced that many sincere Christians want to witness for God, but the question is How can they do their part when they feel extremely uncomfortable speaking one-on-one? Many well-meaning individuals would rather die than get up front on Sabbath and talk about Ingathering, for example. They themselves do not like knocking on doors, so why would anyone else want to do it? Although they would like to share their Christian experience, they freeze at the very thought of standing in front of others.

My wife and I have vastly different temperaments, as different as night and day. She likes quietness; I prefer noise. She wants the windows closed, while I throw them open. For her the toilet paper and paper towel roll should go one way and for me the other. (Everyone knows it should come off from the bottom.) We differ on the style of peanut butter we buy and the milk we drink. Kathy likes soy milk and I like skim milk. My philosophy is that if God wanted us to drink milk from a bean, He would have placed udders on them. Almost everything in our marriage is that way. We are as opposite as two people can be. But through the years of our marriage we have learned to strengthen, enhance, magnify, and support each other in our temperaments.

We proved it again at our 1997 camp meeting. When the conference administration asked me to be the primary leader at camp meeting, I froze. For the past six years I had worked only with the juniors. I liked working in the junior department. The juniors and I clicked. For you see, sanguines never grow up past the junior age. We are just overgrown kids who want nothing more out of life than to have fun! But primary? I'd never worked with that age at camp meeting before, and I didn't know if they knew how to have fun or if I could think at their level. From the small past experience I'd had working with the primary age I thought that all they knew how to do was ask questions about everything in life. Why this? Why that? Why? Why? Why?

Finally I agreed to be the leader on one condition: that Kathy be my assistant. She had worked with that age group before, having been a primary and kindergarten teacher in Sabbath school for years. It would be the only way I would do it. Of course the conference jumped right on that. Two for the price of one. No problem!

Because I was about to start an evangelistic series in my district two months before camp meeting, I turned everything about the primary class over to Kathy. (Wasn't that nice of me?) Her creative, conscientious, and idealistic mind immediately went to work. She started writing letters to almost every employee in the conference, asking if they could tell a story, help in crafts, sing, play the piano, etc. In no time at all she had planned the theme, the songs, the backdrop and props. Then she started collecting and buying baskets, bottles, and anything that looked like it might have come from Bible times. What was I doing? Waiting for her to tell me what to do. My unorganized, forgetful, inconsistent mind was busy doing other things.

But Kathy knew I was there if she needed me. She enjoyed planning the program (knowing that I wouldn't start preparing until one week—or one day—before camp meeting started, and would have no idea what to make my theme). When asked, I collected large boxes to make biblical-style houses out of. I did everything Kathy asked me to do, so please don't think too badly of me.

When we arrived at camp meeting, the two craft women my wife had recruited had their stuff ready also. (Believe it or not, one of them was a melancholy and the other was a sanguine.) They had some of the neatest crafts planned for our primary class. Joining them was one of their church members who played the piano. All week long we worked together with not one misunderstanding, disagreement, or complaint among us. In fact, we meshed so well that our class attendance was more than the conference said we would have. Some of the juniors were coming to our room. Having been in juniors for six years, I know it is usually the other way around. Kathy led the singing, while I did the preaching and told stories using many of my puppets (I'm a ventriloquist). Marilyn and Marilynne told stories and did crafts, and Pat played the piano. Each one of us worked within our own temperament, talent, and personality and allowed the others to work in theirs, helping us to have one of the best primary classes ever. We had mothers and fathers coming day after day, telling us that their children enjoyed their class and that it was all they could talk about. One of the greatest compliments anyone could have given us was when they asked if we were going to be the leaders again next year.

If we could only learn to employ this same idea in our churches and witnessing programs, what a difference it would make.

It is not my purpose to write another book about witnessing, but rather to underscore the things we already know about witnessing. What I want to share with you throughout this entire volume is that our witnessing approaches can be better understood than we have yet to experience. "There is a science of Christianity to be mastered—a science as much deeper, broader, higher than any human science as the heavens are higher than the earth. The mind is to be disciplined, educated, trained; for we are to do service for God in ways that are not in harmony with inborn inclination. There are hereditary and cultivated tendencies to evil that must be overcome. Often the training and education of a lifetime must be discarded, that one may become a learner in the school of Christ. Our hearts must be educated to become steadfast in God. We are to form habits of thought that will enable us to resist temptation. We must learn to look upward. The principles of the word of God—principles that are as high as heaven, and that compass eternity—we are to understand in their bearing upon our daily life. Every act, every word, every thought, is to be in accord with these principles" (*Testimonies for the Church,* vol. 8, p. 314).

Chapter 2

Do You Need a Mulligan in Your Witnessing?

A COUPLE years ago while I lived in Mississippi, a church member bought me the first (and only) set of golf clubs that I've ever owned. One morning he took me out to play a round of 18 holes. Never having played golf before, I knew nothing about the game. Zilch!

The first thing I remember Bill teaching me was how to hold the club. That as I stood I should never take my eye off the ball and should be sure to follow through with my swing. Finally the time came for me to hit my first golf ball. Needless to say, I had a lot of confidence in myself. I had watched it done on television many times, listened to other ministers talk about golf at meetings, and just finished watching Bill hit the ball. Sure, I could do it! No problem.

Now, I could tell that the flag was about 150 yards away from us and doglegged a little to the left. We had a wind about five miles an hour out of the south, so I asked Bill, "With there being water on our right side and a sand trap on the left, what do you think I should use—my orange, white, or yellow ball?"

After Bill laughed for a minute or so and helped me decide which color ball to use, I stood over the tee, placed my eyes on the ball, and started with my swing. Watching and swinging. I just knew I was going to sail that ball over the green and be the first person ever to hit a hole-in-one their first time playing golf.

Well, as my swing came down something must have happened. I believe it was a bird tweeting and another golfer yelling "Fore" that threw me off. I'm not sure what happened, but as I came through with my swing, I missed the ball, put a two-inch hole in the ground, and bent my club. Bill just stood there and laughed at me again. I stepped back, mumbled a few words at that bird and the other golfer, gave Bill one of those looks, and decided to take another try. He attempted to give me a little more advice, but he must have forgotten that I was his pastor and knew everything about golf already because I had watched the pros on television and had listened to many fellow clergy at staff meetings discuss their golf games. Well, I took another swing, and this time I did hit the ball, and it went sailing! In fact, it hurtled through the air so fast that I couldn't even see it. As I stood there looking way down the fairway, Bill tapped me on the shoulder and pointed to my ball two feet in front of me.

Golf is a fun but crazy game. A few years ago someone told me that the name is actually an acrostic for "Game of Looking Foolish!" And friend, I did look foolish playing this sport.

Bill taught me a lot about golf that day, but years later I discovered that Bill forgot to teach me another vital rule of golf—one called a "mulligan." Now, if you are a golf player, you probably have heard about the mulligan. Webster's dictionary defines it as "a free shot sometimes given a golfer in informal play when the previous shot was poorly played."

You use a mulligan when you make a lousy swing as I did my first game and you get to discard that swing. Instead, you have the chance to pull out a new ball and start all over, as if the unlucky shot had never happened. This time you hope and pray that the second stroke is better than the first.

Wouldn't it be great if we could apply the idea of mulligans to all areas of our lives? Picture this. As you drive down the highway and look in your rearview mirror, you see something that makes butterflies hurtle around your stomach. Flashing red or blue lights tell you to pull over. As the officer writes up a ticket and hands it to you, you say, "No thanks, officer, I'm taking a mulligan today!" And you hand it back to him.

Or say you misread the map and travel the wrong road for miles before you realize it. You can then tell your spouse that you "want a mulligan on this trip."

How about the student who flunks a vital test that determines whether they will graduate or not? After receiving the test result, the student simply says, "Teach, I would like to have a mulligan on this test, please."

Or what if a preacher bombs on a sermon? While standing at the door and shaking your hand, they simply say, "I'm taking a mulligan on this sermon today!"

Do you need a mulligan in any area of your life today? Maybe you have some things in your life that you wish you had a second chance at. You want the first time never to have happened. That would be great, wouldn't it?

I can think of a hundred places in my life that I wish I could take a mulligan. But none more than in my witnessing for Jesus. I once heard someone say, "If at first you don't succeed, redefine success." Some of us need to look at our witnessing programs and ask, "Do I need to redefine what a successful witnessing program is?" "Do I need to take a second look at how I personally am witnessing for Jesus?" Always remember that "your success will not depend so much upon your knowledge and accomplishments, as upon your ability to find your way to the heart" (*Gospel Workers,* p. 193).

Our Bible is full of stories of people to whom God gave a second chance. A mulligan, if you please. Something in their life didn't work out the way they had hoped, so God offered them another chance to make things right.

Have you ever wished you had another shot at witnessing to someone you feel you blew it with the first time? You've said something you wished you hadn't, or didn't say something you wished you had? I know I have many times!

Throughout this book I will share with you biblical mulligans and some of my own personal life experiences. I hope they will help you understand how to witness to others in your daily witnessing program for Him.

But before I do, let me tell you that you have to follow certain rules in order to take a mulligan in golf. First, you have to be the one to ask for it. Your friends cannot do it for you. They may suggest you should take one, but you are the only one who can decide to use it. The second rule limits how many mulligans you can have in a single game.

The general rule is only one mulligan for each nine holes. You can't just keep taking them. If that was so, a normal game of golf might last for days. At every swing you might say, "I'll take a mulligan on that one." Then on the next swing, "I'll have another mulligan, please." On and on you use mulligans until you have a perfect game or wear yourself out, whichever comes first. But it just doesn't happen that way. Now, you may be thinking, *Well, great, you talked about taking mulligans in my Christian witnessing, and now you tell me there are limits to how many chances I will get!*

In the Bible rule number one does apply—you have to be the one who decides and asks to have a mulligan (forgiveness). But God waives rule number two. You see, up until shortly before Jesus comes or we die, whichever happens first, God gives us all the chances we need to ask for witnessing mulligans.

If you need a witnessing mulligan today, then ask Jesus to give you one. "Ask, and it shall be given you; seek, and ye shall find; knock, and it shall be opened unto you: for every one that asketh receiveth; and he that seeketh findeth; and to him that knocketh it shall be opened" (Matt. 7:7, 8). It doesn't matter how badly you have witnessed in the past or how many times you have put your foot in your mouth and appeared to have failed God. The Lord wants to give you a witnessing mulligan, and I hope this book will help you toward that second, third, fourth, and so on chance.

Chapter 3

Flying Pizza Witnessing

ONE AFTERNOON when I was managing a pizza restaurant in western Texas, a young man ordered a small onion pizza. After paying for his pizza, he sat down. It was during the middle of the afternoon, and business being slow, he was the only one in the dining room. When the pizza was finished, I called his number. As he approached the counter, I grabbed his pizza plate from the window and turned back toward him so fast that I made his lunch into an instant Frisbee that went flying across the room.

The young man just stood there in amazement as he watched his lunch sail across the tables and land upside down with a huge splat. At first I stood there with my mouth ajar, then immediately started apologizing and offered to give him his money back and make him another fresh pizza. He said that it was OK, that he would just wait for another pizza to be baked, that he wasn't in any hurry, and that he didn't care to have a refund. My mouth gaped wider. Most customers would jump at the opportunity for a free lunch.

After his second pizza came from the oven, I hand-carried it out to him (very slowly) and asked him if I could join him for just a minute; I had a question I wanted to ask. He said that it would be fine, and I sat down with him.

"Please forgive me if I'm wrong. I don't want to offend you," I said, "but are you a Christian?" He quietly said he was, so I quickly replied that he had definitely let his light shine for Jesus and that he was a good example of what true witnessing was all about. Also I told him that he had made a lasting impression on me.

And he did. Listen to what Ellen White once wrote: "How much better it is . . . instead of hearing criticism, to hear from the lips . . . tender and loving words. . . . Such words make lasting impressions" (*Review and Herald,* Sept. 15, 1904). "The Lord Jesus Christ will open the door of their hearts, and will make lasting impressions upon their minds" (*ibid.,* Nov. 23, 1905).

Throughout my years as a Christian witness for Jesus people have told me that my witnessing has been "down to earth." Although my natural temperament is to be kind, considerate, and respectful of others, the truth is that a lot of my witnessing has come from watching and learning from others, such as the individual in the pizza parlor.

One of the greatest challenges of being a Christian is knowing how and when to witness. We often witness, only later to wonder why we didn't say this or that. Or worse yet, why we said whatever we did. I have come to the conclusion that good effective witnessing is knowing what to say, when to say it, and when to keep quiet.

I'm sure that if you are like me, you have at times witnessed to someone only to have them say something like "I just don't understand it the way you do!" At that you want to shake them and say, "Can't you read? It says so right there in the Bible." But that isn't God's way to witness.

During the course of my 20-some years of witnessing I have discovered that no two people think the exact same way. Not married couples, friends, or even church associates. Research in genetics has revealed 300 billion possible chromosome combinations for human beings. That means that every person is truly a one-of-a-kind individual. God must throw away the mold the moment each one of us is born. And since we do not think in the same manner, we often find it hard to witness to others in ways that they can understand.

Because God in His wisdom has allowed each individual to have certain strengths and weaknesses as part of His plan ultimately to bring glory to Himself, we are urged to study *character and manner.* We should study the strengths and weaknesses of different temperaments better to understand ourselves and those to whom God has led us. Ellen White reminds us that "the religion we profess is colored by our natural dispositions and temperaments; therefore it is of the *highest importance* that the *weak points* in our character be *strengthened* by exercise and that the strong, unfavorable *points be weakened by working in an opposite direction* and by strengthening opposite qualities" (*Testimonies for the Church,* vol. 3, p. 504; italics supplied). This applies to those we are studying and witnessing with too. When we discover the strengths and weaknesses of a temperament, we unearth what makes a person tick and how they think. Then hopefully we can apply that knowledge in a way that enables us to help people better understand what God expects from them.

Let me give you a few examples of some of the strengths of the four most commonly recognized temperaments when witnessing or studying with others. If a person has a choleric temperament, then focus on action, provide them with opportunities for autonomy, and offer them a challenge. "They respond positively to the eyesalve of new insights developed into proven spiritual truths. For their sakes, keep the spiritual food on the church plate fresh but identifiable" (Len McMillan, "Feed My Different Sheep," *Ministry,* January 1997, p. 19).

But if the person you are trying to witness to tends to show a strong melancholy disposition, then keep in mind their sensitive, painstaking, idealistic, and creative mind. Melancholies are the most apt to be consistent in their Bible studies with you. Such individuals have a deep need to finish anything they start and seem to like to memorize Bible verses that have a special meaning to them. "They are usually interested in anything that is good for them and, once convinced that they need God, will work tirelessly to become better acquainted with His will" *(ibid.).*

Phlegmatics are usually the most pleasant to witness to. They do not like to argue or disagree with others, which makes them easy to study with. Although witty, they tend to hide their emotions. With their low-key and dependable spirit, they make good listeners, and even if they do not agree with what you have to say, they will stay calm, cool, and collected.

Sanguines will spontaneously react to almost anything a person says, good or bad! They love studying with those who make the learning fun and fulfilling, and they enjoy stories, especially ones with happy endings in which the good guy wins. "If it is immediately enjoyable, sanguines will feed often on the Word of God" *(ibid.,* p. 18). Because they love to talk, let them. If you are enthusiastic and inspiring when studying or witnessing with a sanguine, you will find it will go a long way with them. Even if they don't accept what you show them from God's Word, they will be your friends for life. (We will look much more into witnessing to the different temperaments later.)

Whenever I hear the words "I cannot witness," I ask, "Witness in what way? One-on-one, door-to-door, or regular Bible studies?" Never forget that witnessing does not always have to be in a formal setting. We can witness when someone throws our pizza across the room.

I remember back in the early eighties when the Arkansas-Louisiana Conference decided to try something different during camp meeting one year. They wanted to hold an evangelistic series at the same time camp meeting convened in Shreveport, Louisiana. The first Sabbath during the camp meeting several of us were eating our lunch on the front lawn when evangelist Joe Crews walked by with one of his helpers from the crusade. We each said hello to them as they passed by, but not one of us asked them to join us for lunch. We just knew that they were probably being pulled apart by members begging for them to have lunch with them. Later we found out that not one member had offered them lunch, and they had ended up eating alone in their camper.

When I heard about it, I realized that we had been poor witnesses to them. But I learned a good lesson from that experience! Since that day, if at all possible, my wife and I see to it that whenever any guest visits our church, we invite them to our home for lunch, even if that means opening up another can of Veja-Links.

Often I have looked back at the way I have witnessed in

the past. At times I have walked away from an encounter feeling good about my words and actions. Then at other times I have chastised myself, "Why did I say that?" I know now, only because of past experiences and my personal analysis of witnessing, that if we practiced only a few of the witnessing tips I hope to share with you in this book, we can be much better witnesses for God.

I am writing this book with the notion that you already have a little background in the four temperaments: sanguine, choleric, melancholy, and phlegmatic. But for those who do not and for those who may have forgotten, please allow me to refresh your memory a little about something we each have—our own unique and personal temperament.

Our temperaments influence everything we do, including the way we eat, sleep, work, play, study, and witness. That is why we get along better with some individuals than with others. Or why some children are well behaved and others—well, hopefully you get the point. But one thing is for sure about our temperaments: they never change. We may have the ability to alter our outward appearance from time to time. High-heeled shoes will make us look taller, and we can dye our hair another color. Or perhaps we may wear a mask in front of others to deceive them into believing everything is OK in our life when it really isn't. But our true temperament never changes.

Let me give you an example. Have you ever wondered why your spouse does the things they do? My wife and I for years have gone round and round over my leaving the bathroom commode lid up. She believes and was taught at home that the lid stays down. I, on the other hand, cannot understand what difference it makes. My mother trained me to raise the lid but never bothered to remind me to lower it. I have always operated on the assumption "If I can raise it, she can lower it." But that hasn't seemed to work in our home. So to settle this problem, we live in a house that has what we call his and her bathrooms. (By the way, this is just one of many things we do not see eye-to-eye upon.) Now, I ask, Who is right and who is wrong? And what difference does it make whether the seat is up or down?

By now many of you women readers are asking, "What kind of moron is this author?" (Ouch, that hurt!) "Of course she is right!" At the same time you men are probably saying to yourselves, "Right on. Preach away, brother! Tell those women who's boss!" But the truth is that I forget to place the seat down because of my sanguine temperament. That's not an excuse, just a fact. I would never deliberately leave the seat up knowing that it makes my wife upset.

The basis of this book is not to point out who's right or who's wrong, but to understand why others do what they do and then how we can witness to them. We want to see the way they view the world, to look through their glasses and walk in their shoes.

Let me start by giving you very brief descriptions of the four basic temperaments. We will start with the enthusiastic, talkative, joyful sanguine.

Someone with the sanguine temperament is a warm, lively, buoyant, fun-to-be-with person. Sanguines never go through life unnoticed. Along with the melancholies, they possess the richest emotions of the four basic temperaments. Sanguines are super extroverts and love to be the center of attention. They're the unpredictable driver on any road, liking to speed up and then slow down for no apparent reason. And because they talk a lot with their hands, the passengers in the car with them often become worried. If their teacher were to place each student's desk in a row based on intelligence, the sanguine child usually would not get to sit in the first chair.

I remember one day in grade school back in the sixties. My teacher placed the students' desks in a straight row according to how well they did on their test that week. The classroom had three rows, and she arranged each child in one of the rows starting with the brightest and best-behaved child. She had a row for the smartest, the smart, and the not-so-smart. One day I did really well on a test (well for me, that is) and I took the first chair in the not-so-smart row. I was so happy and excited that I raced home and told my mother, "I was the smartest one in the dumbest group!" My mother still laughs about that to this day.

Sanguines can make good preachers if they learn to time themselves, because their sermons can become a little lengthy. If filled with God's Holy Spirit, they make good spouses. They never lack for friends. Someone once said about a sanguine that "they always enter a room mouth-first." You almost always find them happy and possessing a cooperative, thoughtful, fun-loving, and humorous spirit.

Unfortunately, all temperaments have both strengths and weaknesses, pluses and minuses, and the sanguines have their share. One of their most exposed and unfortunate weaknesses is their lack of discipline. It makes it easy for them to be deceitful, dishonest, and undependable. Sanguines have a tendency to be late for appointments, school, and church. They eat too much and are often overweight. Although voted as "the most likely to succeed," they drop out of school later in life. Weak-willed and undisciplined, they never seem to grow up. Highly emotional, they can easily get hurt by harsh and rash words from others.

Because of their talkative, bubbly spirit, people seem to have a way of excusing their weaknesses by saying, "Oh well, that's just the way they are." I'm sure you know a sanguine or two and at times wish you didn't.

Ellen White's counsel to a sanguine is: "You are of a highly excitable temperament. You have but little self-control and under excitement frequently say and do things which you afterward regret. You should call a determined will to your aid in the warfare against your own inclinations and propensities. . . . You need to cultivate self-control. . . . Discipline yourself to die to self, to bring your will in subjection to the will of Christ" (*Testimonies for the Church,* vol. 4, pp. 214, 215).

The next temperament is the active, strong-willed, independent, self-sufficient, hotheaded, quick-thinking choleric. They often seem to be decisive and opinionated and find it easy to make decisions for themselves and everyone else they know. Full of determination, they love to undertake a challenge. Because they are natural-born leaders, people find it easy to follow them and accept their guidance. When they set their mind to do something (and it doesn't matter what), you can set your watch by it. It will get done. While it may not be as perfect as a melancholy would do it, it will get done. But such individuals do have a down side. They can be extremely bullheaded and determined to get their way.

On one of my trips to Russia I had a person volunteer to join my evangelistic team. I didn't know it at the time but later discovered that the individual had a very strong choleric temperament and couldn't seem to get along with anyone. The volunteer wanted his way and didn't care who got hurt or what he had to say to get it. The person wouldn't listen to reason, and needless to say, it caused a lot of disunity among our team members. The individual's stubbornness destroyed all his good strong points.

Like the sanguines, cholerics are extroverts, just not as intense. They thrive on staying busy. The workaholics of all temperaments, they plan big and set for themselves many goals. Because of their keen minds, they can make sound decisions and many times do so in an instant. Taking strong stands on subjects that interest them, they will stick by their guns through thick and thin. At times they have been considered great opportunists.

Not frightened by misfortune or people, they often have the ability to keep a straight face even when hurting inside. Unable to sympathize easily with others, they have a hard time with those, especially men, who shed any tears. They display little appreciation, if any, for the fine arts.

As my story illustrates, the choleric's greatest weakness is a tendency to be bossy and domineering. They will not hesitate to use any means to accomplish whatever they want. Unless controlled by God's Holy Spirit, they will stomp out of a board meeting when they are not getting their way.

One time while serving as a local elder in a church in Texas, I attended one of those board meetings that you wish you could forget. A highly domineering choleric member wanted something his way, but the board voted him down. That did not sit lightly with him. He became so mad and upset that he stomped out of the room, yelling that he would not be back until the others had seen it his way. It's sad to report, but the board took another vote, and the choleric elder got his way. And what's even sadder is that the same choleric stormed out of the room at still another board meeting a few months later and again forced his will on the others. Knowing that such words and actions brought him the results he wanted, he had learned over the years how to play the "board" game.

We need our choleric leaders. They make excellent ministers. But they must pray daily that the Holy Spirit will guide them and help them to learn to control their temper and tongue.

Ellen White counsels a choleric with these words: "You have not a happy temperament. And not being happy yourself, you fail to make others happy. You have not cultivated affection, tenderness, and love. . . . You are selfish, exacting, and overbearing. . . . You indulge feelings akin to hatred. Your likes and dislikes are strong. . . . You need a fresh conversion every day" (*ibid.,* vol. 1, pp. 694-699).

Next we have the richest of all the temperaments, the melancholy. Melancholies have many fine qualities. Highly analytical, self-sacrificing, gifted, and perfectionistic, with a highly sensitive emotional nature, they receive more enjoyment from the fine arts than any of the four basic temperaments. Introverts, they often slip into different moods.

Melancholy type people can soar to ecstasy, then the next moment plunge into depression. Because of their inclination always to be perfect in everything they do, along with having everyone else be refined, they often find themselves discouraged and disappointed. They have what some like to call the four "isms" that are hard for the other three temperaments to take: skepticism, pessimism, cynicism, and criticism. While the cholerics are hard to please, the melancholies are impossible to satisfy.

I relish spending time with my wife. It seems we don't get enough time with each other as it is, so whenever I can, I enjoy going shopping with her. The only problem I have is that because of her strong melancholy temperament, she will try on an outfit that I may think she looks great in, but if there is one thread out of line or she thinks it makes her look a little big, she will put it back. Then she will find one that she really loves, looks great in, and can afford, but she will want to think about it for a while longer. Me, I walk in, and the first thing that catches my eye I buy. Half the time I don't even try it on until I get home (unless Kathy is with me).

One of the strongest and, in my opinion, the most needed of all strengths is one the melancholies have: the ability to study and understand Scripture as no other temperament can. We need ministers and laypeople who can do that. A melancholy can take almost any verse and dissect it with their logical and analytical mind and explain it better than any of the other temperaments. Also, they can be a perfect idealist if they choose to. But at the same time, because they have to diagnose and analyze everything, they can have some irrational and illogical beliefs. I have one good melancholy friend who loves to study the Bible. But in one area he has come to the conclusion that the Bible says something totally different from the way I, and the church as a whole, for that matter, understand it to say. He is so headstrong about his idea that the Bible means what he says it means and not what the church understands it means that he has left the denomination. It's unfortunate, but along with a strong melancholy temperament he has a strong choleric trait as his second temperament. (We will look more at working with church members and leaders later.)

Ellen White counseled a melancholy this way: "She is naturally quick to see, quick to understand, quick to anticipate, and is of an extremely sensitive nature. . . . She has been disposed to regard everything with a jealous eye, to be suspicious, surmising evil, distrustful of almost everything. This causes unhappiness of mind, despondency, and doubt, where faith and confidence should exist. These unhappy traits of character turn her thoughts into a gloomy channel, where she indulges a foreboding of evil, while a highly sensitive temperament leads her to imagine neglect, slight, and injury, when it does not exist" (*ibid.,* vol. 1, pp. 708, 709).

The last temperament trait is the witty, low-key, dependable, calm, cool, peaceful phlegmatic. They are the ones who like to think before they tackle a job. Natural-born peacemakers, they do not want to argue or have any sort of confrontation with anyone. They would rather negotiate than fight. Their good sense of humor helps see them through tight spots. Highly dependable, they almost always have a cheerful outlook on life. Faithful in fulfilling obligations and always on time for appointments, phlegmatics are extremely practical and efficient. They do not make rash and sudden decisions. Although not perfectionists like melancholies, they often have amazingly high standards of accuracy and precision.

But just like the other three temperaments, they have another side. Some of the phlegmatics' greatest weaknesses are lack of enthusiasm, indecisiveness, shyness, and fearfulness. They hate being hurt or disappointed and can be extremely stubborn at times. Sometimes they will drag their feet when it comes to doing certain things. The world's natural worrywarts, they can become apprehensive about anything and everything.

Because they hate change, you will often find that they are the first ones to complain if the Sabbath school chairs ever get rearranged and they have to sit in a different spot. Liking routine, they seldom ask for anything to be substituted. Their philosophy is "if it ain't broke, don't fix it."

Ellen White wrote to a phlegmatic that "time and strength were devoted to you; and matters were shaped for your special benefit to remove your prejudice and win you to accept the truth, until your indolence and unbelief exhausted the patience of Brother R. This earnest effort on his part you termed crowding and jamming you. Your mulish temperament was manifested; you rose up against this dealing and rejected the efforts he made to help you" (*ibid.,* vol. 2, p. 708).

Well, there you have it. A short rundown of each of the four basic temperaments. Keep in mind that no one temperament is more desirable than another, because each has its own strengths and weaknesses. I haven't yet met anyone who said they would be glad to exchange their temperament for someone else's, especially if the weaknesses of the other temperament come with it. God made us each different, and we can truly say that we are one of a kind. Each has our own strengths and our own weaknesses.

I heard this quote in a seminar once from Len McMillan, from the Pacific Health Education Center in Bakersfield, California: "The melancholy invents a product that is manufactured by the choleric and later sold by the sanguine to be enjoyed by the easygoing phlegmatic."

You will find many good books about temperaments at your local library or at your favorite bookstore. May I suggest you read one or two to learn more on the subject. Because who knows, someday the manager of your favorite pizza place may throw your pizza flying across some restaurant floor and you may want to know how to witness to him or her.

Chapter 4

Understanding Our Temperaments the Down-to-earth Way

THE GOSPEL is too often presented in so indifferent a manner as to make but little impression upon the consciences or the lives of men. . . . The world needs today what it needed nineteen hundred years ago—a revelation of Christ. A great work of reform is demanded, and it is only through the grace of Christ that the work of restoration, physical, mental, and spiritual, can be accomplished. *Christ's method alone will give true success in reaching the people.* The Saviour mingled with men as one who desired their good. He showed His sympathy for them, ministered to their needs, and won their confidence. Then He bade them, 'Follow Me' " (*The Ministry of Healing,* p. 143; italics supplied).

Have you ever noticed that all of us seem to like different material things, different sports, music, books, videos, etc.? We are different in how we drive our cars, the way we do our yards, how our home or office desk looks (glad you can't see mine), the approach we use to study the Bible, the way we enjoy and feel comfortable during church services, and even how we witness.

Do you ever attend church services in which you can't understand the point the pastor is trying to get across? The message just doesn't make a lick of sense to you. It appears to be one of those five-minute sermons prepared on the way to church. Scratching your head, you feel as if you have wasted your time and wish you had just stayed home and watched a video from one of those "good preachers." *This must be the most boring sermon I've ever heard!* you think to yourself. *Surely no one here is receiving any sort of blessing from it.*

Then as you are leaving and about to do your Sabbath duty and shake the pastor's hand, you hear the person in front of you declaring as he or she vigorously pumps the preacher's hand, "Pastor, that had to have been your best sermon ever! I really received a blessing! Thank you." And you stand there doing all you can to keep from laughing. So you graciously shake the pastor's hand and add, "That goes for me too." You feel like a phony, but you believe it was the "Christian" thing to say.

Then you hear the oration-type sermons filled with facts and figures about the money needed to keep the church school operating another year, or that tithe giving is down and we must give until it hurts! Sitting there in your pew, staring straight at the minister, you shake your head, because you cannot believe he or she expects that anyone will receive a Sabbath day's blessing from this sort of reprimand and harangue. Then from behind you comes a voice from Brother Ever-So-Nice shouting, "Amen! Preach on, brother!"

If those examples ring a bell, then I believe you know what I mean when I say that not every sermon is for everyone. Nor will every Bible story fit every individual's personal need. Some speak perfectly to our sinful habits while others do not. Let me give you another example of what I mean.

If you do not have the urge or temptation to have a drink of alcohol every now and then, passages such as Proverbs 20:1 are of not much use to you: "Wine is a mocker, strong drink is raging: and whosoever is deceived thereby is not wise." And if you do not visit a witch or call a television psychic for instructions on how to handle your enemy or find a new love, then the story in 1 Samuel 28 in which King Saul visits the witch of Endor only makes for good reading. Get my point? Not every story or verse will reach every person's specific needs.

I've had people tell me that as a young person growing up they never once struggled with drugs, liquor, or cigarettes. In response I tell them to praise the Lord and give Him all the credit! But I was one of the unfortunate ones who succumbed to this seductive and alluring trap. Even to this day, two decades later, I still have to fight the urge now and then. No doubt you have heard the saying that once you become an alcoholic or drug addict, you will always be one. Some dear saints for some reason or another do not believe that. But let me assure you that it is true.

Because I have walked that road before, I'm able to help many off that particular path to destruction. We need to have more compassion for those who fight battles with liquor, cigarettes, and drugs. Just because a certain sin doesn't tempt or affect you doesn't mean it doesn't lure someone else. I hope you understand my point.

Another area in which people can differ is music. I personally prefer lively toe-tapping music over funeral-type music on Sabbath. I remember a good friend of mine commenting that every Sabbath when he enters the church doors he wonders who died, because he feels as if he just walked into a funeral. But when someone mentioned to the elders that maybe the music could be a little more spirited, the roof almost blew off the church!

Let's consider another sensitive example: hand raising in church. Now, before you get too uptight, I'm not advocating that we raise our hands in church, but when some see others who feel comfortable doing so, they become nervous. Why is that? Isn't it biblical? "I will therefore that men pray every where, *lifting up holy hands,* without wrath and doubting" (1 Tim. 2:8). *"Lift up your hands* in the sanctuary, and bless the Lord" (Ps. 134:2). "We are to come to God, not in a spirit of self-justification, but with humility, repenting of our sins. He is able to help us, willing to do for us more than we ask or think. He has the abundance of heaven wherewith to supply our necessities. 'Every good gift and every perfect gift is from above.' God is holy, and we must pray, *'lifting up holy hands,* without wrath and doubting'" (*Signs of the Times,* Nov. 18, 1903). "Why not pray as though you had a conscience void of offense, and could come to the throne of grace in humility and yet with holy boldness, *lifting up holy hands* without wrath and doubting?" (*Christian Education,* p. 127; italics supplied).

How about our prayers in church? One member prays for every literature evangelist around the world by name. You can tell that the prayers are carefully thought out. The words just musically flow from the lips. Then you have another member who struggles to get just a few words out. The person tries so hard but just can't seem to say what he or she wants to. One individual feels very relaxed praying while another experiences awkwardness.

Remember, I said that no two temperaments are alike. Each of us is a very distinct individual. I'm always telling my wife that when God made her, He threw away the mold. In a sense, that is true. No two of us are exactly alike. Even twins differ in some ways. They may look alike on the outside, but they will not act exactly alike. Their likes and dislikes, their actions and reactions, will vary.

I have a cousin who lives in Texas. He and his wife have a set of twin girls who resemble each other, but their temperaments are as different as night and day. The only way I can tell them apart is that one of them will come up to me the minute I walk in the door and start telling me about her day (a sanguine for sure) and the other will run and hide for a few minutes before she will return to the room I'm sitting in. And even then all she will do is just stare at me (melancholy, no doubt). One is glad I'm there, while the other is asking why I'm there.

Our personality can change over time, depending on our personal circumstances, IQ, occupation, nationality, environment, and upbringing. But even though you can alter your personality, your temperament stays the same. It's the real you.

It's the same with our witnessing. For example, I enjoy preaching to crowds. The more people there, the more merry and relaxed I am. At the same time I tremble at one-on-one witnessing. Don't misunderstand me—I *do* one-on-one witnessing, but that doesn't mean I feel comfortable with it. Does that make me a bad witness for God? I don't think so. Each of us at one time or another has done things that we do not like or feel at ease doing, but we do it anyway.

How about the one who loves to solicit funds door-to-door yet wouldn't think of giving a sermon or a Bible study? Or consider the person who has the talent to play the piano and sing each Sabbath but shies away from teaching Sabbath school. And the list goes on. We are who we are, and we feel the way we feel.

One of the most immense compliments anyone has ever given me came from a friend that I've known since he was 9 years old. (He's in his late 20s now.) He's been a literature evangelist for a number of years now. Recently we were working together when he said, "David, you probably don't know this, but many years ago you helped me find Jesus. You were kind to me and showed me respect even though I was a young kid. I grew up respecting and looking up to you. Thank you for showing me a little of what Jesus is like." It was one of the very few times this sanguine has found himself lost for words.

But it did teach me another lesson about our temperaments. I had treated him the only way I knew how. I wasn't really going out of my way to show Christ to this young kid at the time. Instead, I was just doing what came naturally for me. Now, I'm not saying that I don't have to work at other things, such as controlling my tongue, which is definitely sharper than any double-edged sword. But my natural temperament witnessed to my friend in such a way that he grew up seeing Jesus in me. By the way, he's a sanguine too.

After I started studying into temperaments, I took a survey of my personal one-on-one witnessing and made a phenomenal discovery. Every individual I have ever won to Christ through Bible studies had the same temperament. All were sanguines. *Why is that?* I wondered. Then it dawned on me that I had studied with them in *my* temperament. That was why we had "fun" studying together. Then I considered the ones who didn't make a decision for Christ and join the church, and I realized that they were of different temperaments. I had been trying to get them to see things my way, to view things from a totally different perspective than their own. I wanted them to glimpse Christ from a sanguine's point of view. To look through my glasses and walk in my shoes. Today I realize that is next to impossible to accomplish.

Sometimes Kathy and I would study together on certain subjects and get upset with each other. How could that be, when we both read the exact same passage? Simple—one of us would understand the verse to say something totally different than what the other thought it meant. Other times I would study the Scriptures with fellow pastors, then walk away scratching my head. *How did they get that out of that passage?* I would ask myself. I understood the verses to say something totally different than what they did. Some would see the rules that God commanded us to keep, whereas I might have seen the forgiveness of Christ, or vice versa.

Because of what I have learned about our temperaments, I recognize much better where a person is coming from and why some behave the way they do. Whenever I'm around strong melancholy or choleric pastors who want to study together, I usually will do one of two things—find something else to do or just listen. They will bring their Greek and Hebrew study Bibles, a complete set of commentaries, two or three different versions of the Bible, and volumes of Ellen White, and there I stand with my New King James, thinking, *If God says it, then that settles it for me. Why do we need to do that much study into a verse or a certain word?* Yet many cholerics and melancholies want to dig deep into God's Word, diagram the verse, see what the original Greek or Hebrew said. That's great. We need our deep, thoughtful analytical melancholies and our strong-willed, decisive, goal-oriented cholerics. But all we sanguines want to do is have fun studying God's Word and not get bogged down with words that we can't even pronounce, much less understand.

The peace-loving phlegmatic is probably the easiest of all temperaments to get along with. The closest to being well balanced in everything, they will almost never offend anyone and like to walk the middle of the road in studying with others. While the cholerics are the "born leaders," the phlegmatics are the "learned leaders." They will simply listen while the melancholies, cholerics, and sanguines hash out what Scripture means and say little if anything at all.

Although opposites attract in the way of romance, almost all of our closest friends share the same temperaments as ourselves. They have the same likes and dislikes as we do. When we are dating someone, we usually try to find out what they enjoy and put on an act that we appreciate the same thing too. But the truth is that we only want to be close to them. Then when we get married, we take off the mask and let it be known that we really didn't care that much about what they did.

Let me give you an example. When Kathy and I were dating, I found out she window-shopped. I couldn't care less about shopping. But because I wanted to be with her every waking hour I could, I would offer to take her window-shopping, and we would spend what seemed to me hours and hours just looking at dresses, shoes, purses, even birthday cards at Hallmark. I acted as though I was having fun, and in a way I was, because I was with the one I loved. But what I really wanted to know was what was new in the sports department. What kind of new bicycles, fishing lures, lawn mowers, tools—you know, men stuff. Well, after we got married the truth came out, and needless to say, that didn't fit well with Kathy's melancholy nature. She thought I had lied to her about enjoying shopping. But I hadn't lied—I'd just wanted to be with her.

Doesn't this same thing take place with our witnessing occasionally? We may at first show genuine interest in things others like. We listen to them, ask questions (which I think we should), but later, whether they join the church or not, we sometimes appear to drop them like a hot potato when we start studying or witnessing with someone else. Then they begin to feel that we really didn't care that much about their interests after all. And that kills any of the witnessing progress we may have made.

Ellen White places a great emphasis on having an open and loving relationship with others. "*There is need of coming close to the people by personal effort.* If less time were given to sermonizing, *and more time were spent in personal ministry,* greater results would be seen. The poor are to be relieved, the sick cared for, the sorrowing and the bereaved comforted, the ignorant instructed, the inexperienced counseled. *We are to weep with those that weep, and rejoice with those that rejoice.* Accompanied by the power of persuasion, the power of prayer, the power of the love of God, this work will not, cannot, be without fruit" (*The Ministry of Healing,* pp. 143, 144; italics supplied).

"Herein is my Father glorified, that ye bear much fruit; so shall ye be my disciples" (John 15:8).

An indispensable ingredient of any Christian witnessing involves how we come across to people. How they see us, how we listen to them, how they know we care, and what sort of impact we make on their life. It would be good to remember that "a cold, sunless religion never draws souls to Christ. It drives them away from Him, into the nets that Satan has spread for the feet of the straying" (*Gospel Workers,* p. 478).

As we will see in our next chapter, it is vital to stay close to those we witness to. We must let them know that we care and love them no matter what. Always we need to remember that "the power of Satan now to tempt and deceive is *tenfold greater* than it was in the days of the apostles. His power has increased, and it will increase, until it is taken away. His wrath and hate grow stronger as his time to work draws near its close" (*Spiritual Gifts,* vol. 2, p. 277; italics supplied).

Chapter 5

Remember the Alamo

BORN AND raised a Texan, I take a lot of pride in my home state. The story of the Alamo in San Antonio is one of those things that gives me goosebumps. The rich history of that monument goes back a long time before those fateful 13 days in late February and early March of 1836.

The name "Alamo" comes from a Spanish word meaning "cottonwood." Construction of the two-story stone structure began in 1718 and was completed in 1727. For years it housed priests and served as a place of worship. But then a series of epidemics virtually depopulated most of the Texas missions, and in 1793 civil authorities assumed their functions. The mission era had come to an end.

Shortly after that the Spanish cavalry moved into the abandoned mission and occupied it until Mexican troops took over in 1821. The Spanish cavalry came from Alamo de Parras in Mexico, and the former mission became known as "Pueblo del Alamo." After Mexico won its independence from Spain, Texas in turn sought its independence from Mexico in 1835. General Santa Anna had orders to liquidate the rebellious Texans and convert the mission compound into a fortress at any cost. But inside the Alamo waited 189 men and some women who valued freedom more than life itself. Some were from Gonzales, Texas, having made their way through the Mexican lines in answer to Colonel William Barret Travis's plea for reinforcements. They also included volunteers such as Davy Crockett and his "Tennessee Boys," who owned nothing in Texas and owed nothing to it. In fact, there were men and women there from all over the country that Texas had not a thing to offer but freedom.

For 12 days the 189 individuals withstood the onslaught of a Mexican army that numbered more than 4,000 men. The history books record that Travis unsheathed his sword on the twelfth day during a lull in the virtually incessant bombardment and drew a line on the ground before his battle-weary men. In a voice trembling with emotion he described the hopelessness of their plight and said, "Those prepared to give their lives in freedom's cause, come over to me."

Without hesitation every man but one crossed over the line. Colonel James Bowie asked to have his cot carried over even though he was stricken with pneumonia. Then on March 6, in the chilly predawn morning of the thirteenth day, the bugles of the Mexican soldiers sounded attack. The men inside the Alamo, even though their ammunition and supplies were all but exhausted, continued to resist the Mexican army. Those who perished defending the Alamo that day some 160 years ago died thinking that they had lost the battle. They had fought even though it had seemed hopeless.

What many today do not know is that a victory for the Alamo came 46 days later, on April 21, when some 800 Texans and American volunteers led by General Sam

Houston launched a furious attack on the Mexican army at San Jacinto. As they fought, they shouted, "Remember the Alamo!" They wanted everyone to remember the brave men who had given their lives for freedom, men who had died inside the Alamo thinking they had lost.

"Well," you ask, "what does this have to do with witnessing?" Let me answer by asking you a question. Have you ever heard the words "fight the good fight of faith"? The Bible tells us to "fight" to gain victory. So we "fight" against all odds, waging a battle that seems impossible to win.

We combat sin, and often we struggle hard. And too often we think we have lost because we see no victory. But the truth is we have already won. Jesus fought the battle for us and triumphed many years ago. Although we may feel as if we may never see the victory in our lifetime, the Bible says it's already there. All we must do is accept that God has fought the battle and obtained victory.

Let me tell you a personal story as an example of what I'm trying to say. It involves an evangelistic series I conducted while living in Iowa. Because of all the advertising we did, the series started off with both many members and nonmembers coming. It felt great! In fact, other than some series in Russia, it was the largest attendance of church members and nonmembers combined that I had ever encountered. People had warned me that this part of Iowa was an extremely hard area to evangelize and that one baptism in Iowa was comparable to 10 in other states.

The nightly meetings were to last for four weeks, but we had advertised for only two weeks. As the meeting continued, the attendance of nonmembers started tapering off, but the church members continued to come. They reminded me of the devoted members I found in Russia who showed up night after night no matter what the weather.

By the time the first two weeks had ended, we had lost almost every nonmember, because it was harvesttime. Many of them were farmers and had to tend to their crops. Although I completely understood, I felt greatly disappointed that we had lost so many nonmembers. But we had one man there who did not farm. In fact, he didn't even have a job at the time. Recently he had gone through a divorce and had lost his job, home, and family, and he was hurting badly. Since he had nothing better to do, he decided he would attend the nightly meetings we presented.

Joe knew little about the Seventh-day Adventist Church. But the one thing he noticed right at first was that we were loving people. We loved him for who he was. It didn't matter that he was a man without a job and had little to offer. Nor did we hold it against him that he had recently gone through a divorce. He observed that we believed that he was a child of God and someone important to Him and us. To this day I believe that is what kept him coming more than the message I presented.

To make a long story short, Joe was the only person we baptized. But I would rather have one like him than a hundred others. Not only did Joe completely turn his life over to God, he started telling his friends and relatives about Jesus and His saving grace. Here is another statement from Ellen White: "There is great need of zealous, disinterested workers in God's cause. *One Christ-loving, devoted member will do more good in a church than one hundred half-converted, unsanctified, self-sufficient workers.* It is impossible for the church to be a living, active church unless its members shall be willing to bear burdens and assume responsibilities. *In church relationship are brought together different temperaments and dispositions.* In the _____ church there are a few devoted, God-fearing, faithful souls who pray much, who carry the burden of the church, and whose happiness is in the prosperity of its members" (*Testimonies for the Church,* vol. 5, p. 114; italics supplied).

Joe brought with him his many talents and took to heart the Great Commission of Matthew 28:18-20: "Jesus came and spake unto them, saying, All power is given unto me in heaven and in earth. Go ye therefore, and teach all nations, baptizing them in the name of the Father, and of the Son, and of the Holy Ghost: teaching them to observe all things whatsoever I have commanded you: and, lo, I am with you alway, even unto the end of the world. Amen."

The man became what Matthew 5:14-16 calls "a light of the world": "Ye are the light of the world. A city that is set on an hill cannot be hid. Neither do men light a candle, and put it under a bushel, but on a candlestick; and it giveth light unto all that are in the house. Let your light so shine before men, that they may see your good works, and glorify your Father which is in heaven."

Not only did he turn out to be a faithful church member, he also became one of my closest friends. He was the only person my wife's dog would make friends with and allow to pet him. Joe watched our dogs for the two months we were in Russia and whenever we were out of town. I can't say enough about this dear friend. I know that God has used and will continue to use him to help finish the work that He has given to us. Joe became one of those prepared to take God's message to a dying world. "The last rays of merciful light, the last message of mercy to be given to the world, is a revelation of His character of love. The children of God are to manifest His glory. In their own life and character *they are to reveal what the grace of God has done for them." (Christ's Object Lessons,* pp. 415, 416; italics supplied). *"All who are consecrated to God will be channels of light.* God makes them His agents to communicate to others the riches of His grace. His promise is, 'I will make them and the places round about my hill a blessing; and I will cause the shower to come down in his season; there shall be showers of blessing.' Ezekiel 34:26" (*The Desire of Ages,* p. 141; italics supplied).

Even after Joe joined the church he was still going though some rough times in his life. He didn't know which way to turn. Many times we talked about dying to self and giving to Jesus all that he had and committing his life fully to Jesus. We prayed together, asking God to bless him, and God heard our prayers. He found a good job at Wal-Mart with no Sabbath problems and started being faithful in his tithing. It seemed that the more he gave to God, the more God gave back to him. Soon he found a nice apartment to live in. Then it wasn't long until he got to visit with his children.

Joe discovered what Paul meant when he said we must die to self before we can gain the victory. He realized that is where the victory is found—dying daily to self. My good friend learned that it's not the slipup now and then that can keep a person down. Rather, it is not recognizing the fact that the battle is already won. When Joe accepted Jesus and His saving grace, he also acknowledged the fact that Jesus had already fought his battle for him and won.

Going back to the Alamo story, we find that still others

died fighting for Texas' independence than just those at the Alamo and San Jacinto. These men perished after the battles were over and victory already secured. They died to preserve that triumph. Compare that to why Paul died daily. He wanted to hold on to that victory.

Texas accepted men from all over the country. It did not matter what color they were, what state they came from, or what their past record showed. If they were willing to fight, then Texas wanted them. I have not been able to find in any Texas history books that anyone was turned away for any reason. Nor can I find evidence that the Alamo's defenders turned against each other while inside its walls. They fought side by side. But we as Christians, even though we are inside the walls of God's church, sometimes fight against God. How, you ask? Simply by not accepting the victory already achieved. How and when was the victory won? Again the story of the Alamo gives us an answer.

Every day they would spend time in the morning going over the plans of defense for that day. The solders listened to their commanders. They knew the armies of General Santa Anna were building up. So they got down on their knees and with a stick drew in the sand how they would defend the fort. Each of them realized that they were much safer inside than outside those walls. Surrender was never an option, and the lesson we must learn is that we can never surrender to the enemy. Just as the brave men gave their wills to their commanders, so we too must surrender our will, our allegiance, to our Commander, Jesus Christ.

We need to spend time on our knees in the morning listening to our Commander as He prepares our daily strategy. We know that an army of evil angels waits outside the walls of our defenses, and they want in. But unlike the Alamo, Satan's evil army cannot penetrate our defenses. If we have Christ in our hearts, then our walls are solid, bulletproof, dartproof, and lionproof.

But, you say, they lost the battle at the Alamo. No they didn't. The victory just came later. And while we might not see our victory today, it will happen. The Bible tells us that God will shield us against anything the devil may throw at us. "The God of my rock; in him will I trust: he is my shield, and the horn of my salvation, my high tower, and my refuge, my saviour; thou savest me from violence" (2 Sam. 22:3). "Every word of God is pure: he is a shield unto them that put their trust in him" (Prov. 30:5).

"*It may appear that Satan is triumphant* and that truth is overborne with falsehood and error; *the people over whom God has spread His shield,* and the country which has been an asylum for the conscience-oppressed servants of God and defenders of His truth, may be placed in jeopardy. But God would have us recall His dealings with His people in the past to save them from their enemies. He has always chosen extremities, *when there seemed no possible chance for deliverance from Satan's workings,* for the manifestation of His power. *Man's necessity is God's opportunity*. It may be that a respite may yet be granted for God's people to awake and let their light shine. If the presence of ten righteous persons would have saved the wicked cities of the plain, is it not possible that God will yet, in answer to the prayers of His people, hold in check the workings of those who are making void His law? Shall we not humble our hearts greatly before God, flee to the mercy seat, and plead with Him to reveal His mighty power?"

(Testimonies for the Church, vol. 5, p. 714; italics supplied).

Texans longed for their independence, their freedom from Mexico, but Mexico wanted to fight for what they thought belonged to them. And the devil thinks we are his—but Jesus now owns us. Jesus fought and died to buy our freedom from sin. "Know ye not that . . . ye are not your own? For ye are bought with a price" (1 Cor. 6:19, 20). And what a price! Not "with corruptible things, as silver and gold, . . . but with the precious blood of Christ" (1 Peter 1:18, 19). "Being then made free from sin, ye became the servants of righteousness. I speak after the manner of men because of the infirmity of your flesh: for as ye have yielded your members servants to uncleanness and to iniquity unto iniquity; even so now yield your members servants to righteousness unto holiness. For when ye were the servants of sin, ye were free from righteousness. What fruit had ye then in those things whereof ye are now ashamed? for the end of those things is death. But now being made free from sin, and become servants to God, ye have your fruit unto holiness, and the end everlasting life" (Rom. 6:18-22). And just as the Texans had to accept their independence from Mexico, we Christians have to receive our independence and freedom from sin in God.

It doesn't matter what you have done in the past, what state or country you are from, what color you are or language you speak. God loves and wants you in His army. "Remember the Alamo" and the men who died for our freedom, but more important, let us always remember the God who died and gained our freedom and independence from Satan. As the men of San Jacinto ran yelling "Remember the Alamo," we need to race with the same perseverance, proclaiming "Remember the cross!" We need to fight (witness) for our Lord everyplace He sends us, whether it be in our local neighborhood, across our city or state, or beyond the great seas.

"Take up the work anywhere and everywhere. Do that which is the nearest to you, right at your own doors, however humble and uncommended it may seem. Work only for the glory of God and the good of men. Let self sink out of sight, while with earnest purpose and solemn prayers of faith you work for Him who has died that you might live. Go to your neighbors one by one, and come close to them till their hearts are warmed by your unselfish interest and love. Sympathize with them, pray for them, *watch for opportunities to do them good,* and as you can, gather a few together and open the word of God to their darkened minds. *Keep watching, as he who must render an account for the souls of men, and make the most of the privileges that God gives you of laboring with him in his moral vineyard.* Do not neglect speaking to your neighbors, and doing them all the kindness in your power, that you 'by all means may save some.' We need to seek for the spirit that constrained the apostle Paul to go from house to house, pleading with tears, and teaching 'repentance toward God, and faith toward our Lord Jesus Christ'" (*Review and Herald,* Mar. 13, 1888; italics supplied).

We need to fight the good fight of faith because we are free to live and witness to others. Fight for the freedom to witness for Jesus just as those at the Alamo struggled for their freedom.

Ellen White stated emphatically that God holds us responsible for witnessing to our neighbors and the world.

"Behold the cities, and their need of the gospel! The need of earnest laborers among the multitudes of the cities has been kept before me. . . . Who are carrying a burden for the large cities? A few have felt the burden, but in comparison with the great need and the many opportunities but little attention has been given to this work" (*Testimonies,* vol. 9, pp. 97, 98).

God has chosen us to carry His message to the cities. We must witness to our family and friends as well as our neighbors. If Jesus is coming as soon as we believe and preach, ought we not to be doing our best to tell others of His love and forgiveness, ought we not to be warning of the destruction that looms ahead of us? Yet most of us become paralyzed at the thought of witnessing door-to-door. So we run away as Jonah did when God sent him to Nineveh. Why not accept that the battle has been fought and won for each of us?

If I said you could witness to others in a way comfortable to you, would you then be more willing? Then keep reading, because we are getting there. But first, I believe what we need is a better understanding of our personal spiritual gifts. We will discuss them in our next chapter.

Chapter 6

Your Temperament and Spiritual Gifts

Most likely you have heard a lot about spiritual gifts lately. We had a whole quarter of Sabbath school lessons on them recently. In it we discovered that each of us has one or more spiritual gifts. Just what spiritual gifts we each possess is a question we must answer for ourselves. If you do not know what your spiritual gifts are, may I suggest you call your local Adventist Book Center and ask what they have available on the topic. The church and others have published many good books on knowing and understanding what our spiritual gifts are. But in this chapter I would like to examine how our spiritual gifts, talents, and temperaments can work together.

Spiritual gifts may or may not match our inherited talents and temperaments. Our spiritual gifts may develop through education, job skills, and hobbies. We must also keep in mind that sometimes the Holy Spirit assigns certain gifts that will match our personality profile and sometimes not. God has given us spiritual gifts for one reason only, and that is to advance His kingdom. First Corinthians 12:12-27 illustrates how our individual spiritual gifts usually work best when used alongside our talents and temperaments. Paul describes how the body works together both as individual parts and in unity with each other.

The Seventh-day Adventist fundamental beliefs declare that "God bestows upon all members of His church in every age spiritual gifts which each member is to employ in loving ministry for the common good of the church and of humanity. Given by the agency of the Holy Spirit, who apportions to each member as He wills, the gifts provide all abilities and ministries needed by the church to fulfill its divinely ordained functions. According to the Scriptures, these gifts include such ministries as faith, healing, prophecy, proclamation, teaching, administration, reconciliation, compassion, and self-sacrificing service and charity for the help and encouragement of people. Some members are called of God and endowed by the Spirit for functions recognized by the church in pastoral, evangelistic, apostolic, and teaching ministries particularly needed to equip the members for service, to build up the church to spiritual maturity, and to foster unity of the faith and knowledge of God. When members employ these spiritual gifts as faithful stewards of God's varied grace, the church is protected from the destructive influence of false doctrine, grows with a growth that is from God, and is built up in faith and love" (*Seventh-day Adventist Yearbook* [1998], pp. 6, 7).

I remember shopping for a suit one day. I had lost some 30 pounds and my clothes just hung on me. Because I would be needing several suits, someone told me about a place not too far from us that had many good used suits at reasonable prices. One afternoon I decided to check the place out. They did have numerous suits—in fact, too many. So many suits crowded the racks that I couldn't see what they had. And of course they were not grouped according to size, so I had to look at them one at a time until something caught my eye. But I was sure that there was a suit somewhere on that rack for me.

I found some very expensive suits from Rome and Italy that interested me, but they were either too big or too small. Every suit that I liked didn't seem to fit just right, and I didn't care for the color or style of the ones that did fit. I tried on suits that I could tell probably came from Wal-Mart and some that appeared to be from expensive men's stores. After spending some time there, I got tired, gave up, and ended up not buying anything at all. The place had just too many to choose from, and I felt tension and pressure building up inside me. Although I had expected to find a suit, I left because the choice was just too great.

I believe that is how our temperament, talent, and gifts can work too if we are not careful. We each have different capabilities and gifts that God gave us as well as some learned ones as well. Gifts that God expects us to use to help finish His work. But we have to understand and accept that not every talent will fit every person's needs in witnessing. In addition, not every gift will reach the same people. There may be people that only a person with that same temperament can reach. The resale shop had so many suits for me to choose from that it became confusing. Just as suits come in different shapes and sizes, so do temperaments, gifts, and talents.

If we place too much knowledge before someone too soon—in other words, give them too much to choose from—it too can be confusing. At the same time, if we do not give them a choice of some sort, it also can be a problem. Some people like one slice of pie at a time. Few people can eat the whole pie at one sitting. Unless we understand how much of the pie (witnessing) people can handle at any time, we stand a good chance of confusing them, even to the point that they either stop eating (studying) altogether or they never accept the gospel truths we present. But how do we know the difference? How do we know when to speak and when to remain silent? I hope to answer that question throughout this book.

Why is it that sometimes we place undue pressure on people we witness to, hoping to persuade them to see things our way? I've gone with some members who tried to witness in ways that they themselves would have resented. I guess they forgot what Matthew 7:12 says: "Whatever you want men to do to you, do also to them, for this is the Law and the Prophets" (NKJV). Unless we understand the temperament of the one we seek to reach, problems may arise. Often that is why it's hard to get some individuals to make a decision to accept the Sabbath command, or any other belief, for that matter. We naturally teach them in ways that we understand and can communicate. It is difficult to explain things in a way they can comprehend, since we have a different temperament and thus do not think in the same manner they do. To us it may be clear what we are trying to say, but to others we do not make any sense.

Sometimes it's hard to understand why a person never makes the decision to join the church or to accept Jesus. But Ellen White reminds us that "we all need to *study character and manner* that we may know how to deal judiciously with different minds, that we may use our best endeavors to help them to a correct understanding of the word of God and to a true Christian life. . . . The person must be shown his true character, understand his own peculiarities of disposition and temperament, and see his infirmities" (*Testimonies for the Church*, vol. 4, p. 69; italics supplied). In order to do that, we first must understand the temperaments ourselves.

After years of studying and praying about this matter, I have concluded that when we witness to those of a different temperament than ours, miscommunication arises, and we will find it very difficult—at times impossible—to convey what we are trying to help them understand and accept.

Let me give you an example from a personal experience. The last Sabbath before we left Iowa I had the privilege of baptizing two women, Martha and Kaye, in a lake. They both had become close friends of Kathy's and mine.

Martha had grown up as a Seventh-day Adventist but had wandered away and would attend church only every now and then. Kaye and her daughter, Sharon, had come in through an evangelistic series before I became the pastor. (I had already baptized Sharon a few months earlier.) During her life Martha had gone through many ups and downs. She confessed to me that she really loved Jesus but had never really known Him as her personal Saviour. Different pastors would visit her and invite her back to church. She would attend off and on but never felt at home because she sensed that people just didn't understand her situation. Then God moved Kathy and me there, and "it was *like* at first sight."

Later she told me that my western Texas drawl attracted her some. She loved to hear me say certain words because they made her laugh and feel good inside. (Even accents can witness for God). Then she and the other two women asked if I would study with them. As I did so, I explained God's never-ending love and forgiveness to them the way I understood it.

At first they had a hard time accepting the fact that God loved them and would be pleased to forgive their past. I stressed that God loved them even though they were still smoking. All three had a problem with tobacco, and being a former smoker myself, I had walked in their shoes. I was able to understand what they were going through. After a while Martha and Sharon managed to quit smoking. Kaye tried and did quit for some time, but the old habit kept coming back. (More on why old habits return easier to some than to others in the chapter "How to Witness to a Sanguine.") With time, love, patience, God's help, and much prayer, all three succeeded in breaking the habit once and for all.

Not too long after we met we started playing gospel music together. Daily I watched all three of them grow in Christ; they gave their hearts to Him fully. Besides having the honor of baptizing them, I also had the privilege of marrying Sharon to a man named Gary. She had been witnessing to him at work. Over time he too gave his heart to the Lord. (More on this subject in the chapter "The Domino Effect.")

It wasn't until I was studying for my master's and doctoral degrees in Christian counseling and psychology that I realized why God was able to use me to witness to the three women in such a way that they joined the church when they did. Why weren't the former pastors able to reach them? Well, the answer is quite simple. We each had some sanguine temperament in us. It was easy for me to witness to them, and that is why we seemed to click. All of us had similar likes and dislikes. We were interested in the same verses of the Bible, we enjoyed the same kind of music, and we weren't afraid to get up front and share our talents through special music.

After their baptism that Sabbath afternoon, the three women and church gave us one of the sweetest going-away ceremonies Kathy and I had ever attended. They even wrote a number entitled "Pastor Farmer's Song" and sang it to us. I have a copy hanging on the wall in my office. Kathy and I both left with tears in our eyes that day. Of course, not every member of that congregation was a sanguine. In fact, in church you will find fewer sanguines than any other temperament. They are the easiest targets for Satan's traps. (See the chapter "How to Witness to a Sanguine.") But through the years, using the principles I'm sharing with you, I have been able to minister to my members in each of their own temperaments. In fact, I was doing that before I became a minister or even understood what the temperaments were all about. It just seemed to come to me naturally. Perhaps it was one of those spiritual gifts. We will look more into how to witness to different temperaments later.

The apostle Paul has a lot to say about witnessing within your temperament, talent, and spiritual gifts. He may not have employed those words, but I believe that was what a lot of his message conveyed. Listen to 1 Corinthians 9:16-24: "Though I preach the gospel, I have nothing to glory of: for necessity is laid upon me; yea, woe is unto me, if I preach not the gospel! For if I do this thing willingly, I have a reward: but if against my will, a dispensation *of the gospel* is committed unto me. What is my reward then? Verily that, when I preach the gospel, I may make the gospel of Christ without charge, that I abuse not my power in the gospel. For though I be free from all men, yet have I made myself servant unto all, that I might gain the more. And *unto the Jews I became as a Jew*, that I might gain the Jews; to them that are under the law, as under the law, that I might gain them that are under the law. . . . *To the weak became I as weak*, that I might gain the weak: *I am made all things to all men*, that I might by all means save some. And this I do for the gospel's sake, that I might be partaker thereof with you. Know ye not that they which run in a race run all, but one receiveth the prize? So run, that ye may obtain."

Paul had learned to read and understand others and knew the penalty of being silent. That is why he felt compelled to preach the gospel wherever he traveled. He recognized that God had commissioned him to travel and announce glad tidings of deliverance from sin to everyone he met. But if he remained silent, he would never find true peace of mind, true happiness, and pure communion with Christ. Also, he knew that to remain silent would have meant to deny the charge the Lord had given him. Today God has called every Christian to be a witness and spread the gospel to everyone they meet. "There is an individual work for each one to do" (*Signs of the Times*, Aug. 21, 1884).

No true born-again Christian should ever be satisfied with just everyday activity. They should not be happy or content unless they are telling others about Jesus. Each should have a clear conscience and peace of mind when they witness. Daily, like Paul, we must be on our knees, asking God to give us the desire to share our testimony with others. "It is the privilege of every soul to be a living channel through which God can communicate to the world the treasures of His grace, the unsearchable riches of Christ. There is nothing that Christ desires so much as agents who will represent to the world His Spirit and character. There is nothing that the world needs so much as the manifestation through humanity of the Saviour's love. All heaven is waiting for channels through which can be poured the holy oil to be a joy and blessing to human hearts" (*Christ's Object Lessons,* p. 419).

Witnessing for Jesus and spreading the gospel is the most important calling in the world. We must let the Holy Spirit guide us, and consider witnessing a sacred duty. Christians must do even more than appears necessary because they love the Lord and appreciate the value of others. God's followers should be impelled by an inward sense of urgency to seek and to save lost men and women. Jesus commissioned all who believe in Him to witness for Him. "Jesus came and spake unto them, saying, All power is given unto me in heaven and in earth. Go ye therefore, and teach all nations, baptizing them in the name of the Father, and of the Son, and of the Holy Ghost: teaching them to observe all things whatsoever I have commanded you: and, lo, I am with you alway, even unto the end of the world. Amen" (Matt. 28:18-20). All who love the Saviour will respond to that commission by permitting the Holy Spirit to shine through them to whomever they come in contact with.

We should not witness grudgingly or unwillingly, but consider it a privilege. When Paul received his call, he gladly accepted his responsibility. Denying himself many comforts and conveniences, he subjected himself to hardship and toil to support himself while preaching the gospel and witnessing. Time after time he demonstrated that his heart was in his work and that he really enjoyed and loved it.

Acutely aware of the pain he had caused Christ and His followers, even though he had sincerely believed that he was carrying out God's will, he recognized the mercy that God gave him and the great trust placed in him. Gladly he accepted his call and commission. Overwhelmed and full of love, he gave all he had to the gratifying task of taking the message of salvation to all, Jews and Gentiles alike. He was willing to labor and witness to others as a slave does, without reward or pay. The apostle would do almost anything to advance their welfare. Observing their habits, customs, and opinions, as far as possible, without compromising principle, he adopted their customs. As God's people, we must be willing to adapt ourselves and our ministry to the nature of those God sends us to.

Paul subjected every goal and course in his life to preaching the gospel and winning others for Christ. The apostle desired that the Holy Spirit would use him to witness to the greatest number possible and to help them accept salvation. It should be the same ambition of every true follower of Christ today.

Not only did Paul adapt his preaching to the Jews, he also seemed to conform to their customs. Being a former Pharisee and a member of the Sanhedrin, he was well aware of their ways. Such knowledge helped Paul witness to and evangelize the Jews. He submitted to their practices and ideas as far as he could and still keep a clear conscience. Not wanting to offend any of them unnecessarily, he attempted to use his awareness of their beliefs and customs in such a way that made it easier for him to demonstrate the gospel to them. I believe his whole purpose in adjusting to their belief was to lead them to Christ.

But Paul never compromised God's laws or principles. He was very careful about that. When Jewish leaders accused him of being a traitor to his people and faith, he would state that he had kept the laws and customs of the Jews when and where he could. Paul had a desire to win every person possible to Christ. Jesus had set the example of adjusting oneself to the customs of others. Adaptability is one of the most useful features that Christians can develop. It helps them to work as Jesus did and to witness as He witnessed. We should, like Jesus, witness in the homes of the poor and illiterate, the wealthy, in the offices, in the market, and everywhere God sends us. Each of us should be willing to go anywhere at any time, and use whatever technique or method that is most suitable for us, whether it be the approach found in this book or whatever else works best for you. Our goal should be to win men, women, and children for God's eternal kingdom.

Paul was so conscious of the reality of Jesus' love, the fact of His resurrection, and the truth of God's mercy, that he found himself driven by a desire to save others no matter what the cost to himself. It must be our experience as the Holy Spirit leads us too. Dying to self daily, we must share the joy of the promise of eternal life with others.

I coined an expression a long time ago that has helped me tremendously in my witnessing. It goes something like this: "I will not bring God down to our level, but I will come down to almost any level and bring them up to God's." As Christians who want to witness for God, we should be willing to go anyplace God sends us. "Christ's commission, 'Go ye into all the world, and preach the gospel to every creature,' is spoken to every one of His followers. All who are ordained unto the life of Christ are ordained to work for the salvation of their fellow-men. Their hearts will throb in unison with the heart of Christ. The same longing of soul that He felt will be manifest in them. *Not all can fill the same place in the work, but there is a place and a work for all.* All upon whom God's blessing has been bestowed are to respond by actual service; *every gift is to be employed for the advancement of His kingdom and the glory of His name" (Australasian Union Conference Record,* June 1, 1904; italics supplied).

If we learn to work within our temperament along with using our God-given spiritual gifts, we will find that we are able to improve our witnessing and accomplish much more for God. Our spiritual gifts, unlike temperaments, can change. Even if you have had a test on spiritual gifts in the past, take another. You may find that your spiritual gifts have changed during the years. Mine did. Ten years ago I scored high in hospitality. Today faith and leadership rank at the top. I believe the change occurred because of my work as a pastor. God strengthened a gift that I had been weak in years ago.

Chapter 7

Back From Failure

PERSONALITY IS the ingrained pattern of behavior, thoughts, and feelings consistent across situations and time. Although we tend to act differently depending upon whom we are talking to, there are certain tendencies in behavior and thinking which persist regardless of the situation or person" (*Introduction to Psychology and Counseling,* p. 225).

"When they had dined, Jesus saith to Simon Peter, Simon, son of Jonas, lovest thou me more than these? He saith unto him, Yea, Lord; thou knowest that I love thee. He saith unto him, Feed my lambs. He saith to him again the second time, Simon, son of Jonas, lovest thou me? He saith unto him, Yea, Lord; thou knowest that I love thee. He saith unto him, Feed my sheep. He saith unto him the third time, Simon, son of Jonas, lovest thou me? Peter was grieved because he said unto him the third time, Lovest thou me? And he said unto him, Lord, thou knowest all things; thou knowest that I love thee. Jesus saith unto him, Feed my sheep. Verily, verily, I say unto thee, When thou wast young, thou girdest thyself, and walkest whither thou wouldest: but when thou shalt be old, thou shalt stretch forth thy hands, and another shall gird thee, and carry thee whither thou wouldest not. This spake he, signifying by what death he should glorify God. And when he had spoken this, he saith unto him, Follow me" (John 21:15-19).

Not long ago I ran across a newspaper cartoon that depicted Dennis the Menace kneeling by his bed, saying his prayers. He had his hands folded and was looking toward heaven. But he was also wearing his pajamas, cowboy hat, cowboy boots, and his six-shooter strapped to his side. The caption read: "I'm Here to Turn Myself In!"

Have you ever been in Dennis's shoes, telling God you blew it? You feel guilty because you have failed Him again, for what you believe to be the millionth time this month!

Failure is a painful word. Some may feel that they have made a mess of their job. Others may feel they have blown it in school or in raising their children. But probably the worst feeling is that we have disappointed God. And we all know that spiritual failure is often devastating. We worry that we have really let God down to the point that He's probably had it and is through with us. So after a long period of guilt we drop to our knees and plead with God to forgive us and give us the strength we will need never to do that same sin again.

The word failure can turn us red inside and out. Many of us have felt like losers when we have tried to witness for our Lord. Once I heard someone say that there are three things about our Bible that everyone needs to know. First, God wrote it. "All scripture is given by inspiration of God, and is profitable for doctrine, for reproof, for correction, for instruction in righteousness" (2 Tim. 3:16).

Second, when we read His book, we find that He included many stories about people who failed. In fact, some succumbed repeatedly, as we see in accounts of Jonah,

Peter, John, David, Samson, and so on. Now if you or I had been writing the Bible, we probably would have left out all the incidents in which people failed, wouldn't we? After all, they were God's people. And just like the 18 minutes missing from the Watergate tapes, we would not have wanted the world to know about the people who had problems during Bible times. Since they were supposed to have been saints, we would have covered the truth up as so many Communist countries did for years.

Third, the Bible also tells about the God who wrote it. The central theme of the entire Bible reveals a God full of love and grace. "Thou, O Lord, art a God full of compassion, and gracious, longsuffering, and plenteous in mercy and truth" (Ps. 86:15). A God who sent His Son to rescue humanity. "God sent not his Son into the world to condemn the world; but that the world through him might be saved" (John 3:17). He is a God who forgives human failure. "Who forgiveth all thine iniquities" (Ps. 103:3). We must understand something at this point: just because He is a God of love and grace does not give any of us license to sin! And just because He forgives us doesn't mean we can go on living the way we have in the past. But we can be thankful that He understands us. We can be grateful knowing that He works on the broken and wounded as well. Be thrilled that He never gives up on us. We may lose hope in ourselves, but God never abandons any of us.

Do you remember the story by the sea in Luke 5? In verse 8 we find Simon Peter telling Jesus to go away, because the disciple is a sinful man. In other words, Peter was saying, "Lord, do not waste Your time on a bum like me." Peter had experienced failure. Have you ever expressed those same words to God? "Lord, don't waste Your time on a bum like me." But did you really want God to quit working on you? Of course not. And neither did Peter. Commenting on the verse, Ellen White said, "Peter exclaimed, 'Depart from me; for I am a sinful man;' yet he clung to the feet of Jesus, feeling that he could not be parted from Him" (*The Desire of Ages*, p. 246). We must ourselves learn to cling to the feet of Jesus and not let Him go.

When Peter denied Christ for the third time, God used an animal to show Peter his failure. And often God employs different ways to reveal our lack of success. When you get right down to it, the passage from John 21 that we looked at in the beginning of this chapter doesn't deal with Peter's failure, but rather the disciple's coming back from it. Ellen White commented that "temporary failure should make us lean more heavily on Christ, and we should press on with brave heart, determined will, and unfaltering purpose" (*Signs of the Times*, Aug. 14, 1884).

In my NIV Serendipity Bible the heading above the passage in John 21 reads: "Jesus Reinstates Peter." Can Peter make a comeback? After all, he has blown it time after time with his Master. Can he this time stand up and walk right with the Lord? Remember, three times he has denied knowing Jesus. And here we find Jesus asking Peter three times if he loves Him.

By the time Jesus asked the same question the third time, Peter was very grieved (verse 17). The repeated questions vividly brought Peter's shameful denials back to his mind. They wounded Peter just like a barbed arrow stabbing through his heart. But as Jesus asked Peter the same question three times, the disciple showed himself to be fully sorry and repentant. Now Jesus could entrust him with His flock. So Peter came back from a certain failure and made a great impact on the growing church of God (see *The Seventh-day Adventist Bible Commentary,* vol. 5, p. 1072).

When I first entered the ministry I worked as a Bible instructor in a small city in Mississippi. My heart and soul had always been in evangelism. So during each of the three years I gave two Daniel and Revelation seminars and one full evangelistic series. But we didn't have even one baptism. The only good thing that seemed to come from the series was that a young married couple attended all three sessions.

At first I was extremely depressed and felt as if I had let God down. I had really tried hard to help those coming to accept Christ, but nothing seemed to work. Then suddenly I received a request from the General Conference for me to form a team, travel to Russia, and conduct a five-week evangelistic campaign. At first I was ecstatic and overjoyed, but then after a while reality set in. I questioned God. "Why me?" I kept saying again and again. "But Lord, I'm only a Bible instructor, and we haven't had any baptisms from our endeavors here!" But to make a long story short, we went and baptized 78 people. Since then we have traveled back a second time and discovered that many of those baptized the first trip have brought others into God's fold. (In the chapter "The Domino Effect" we will look more into the subject of new converts winning others.)

Shortly after Kathy and I returned from Russia, we received an offer to enter the ministry full-time and moved to Iowa to pastor a three-church district. While there we received word that the couple who had attended the three series of meetings in Mississippi had accepted Christ and joined the church. That convinced me that no matter what we do for the Lord, it is never in vain. We cannot do anything for God and fail as long as we allow Him to lead! "As you regard your eternal interest, arouse yourselves, and begin to sow good seed. That which you sow, you shall also reap. The harvest is coming—the great reaping time, when we shall reap what we have sown. *There will be no failure in the crop; the harvest is sure*. Now is the sowing time. Now make efforts to be rich in good works, 'ready to distribute, willing to communicate,' laying up in store for yourselves a good foundation against the time to come, that ye 'may lay hold on eternal life'" (*Testimonies for the Church,* vol. 2, p. 31; italics supplied).

Do you realize that when you look at Jesus' life and ministry while He was here on earth, you might consider Him a failure? Think about it for a moment. He had only 12 men in His primary congregation to work with. They heard Jesus' same sermons again and again and lived with Him for three and a half years. But even with all that time together, not one really grasped the message He sought to teach them and the world. Not one of them really understood Jesus when He spoke about His death, burial, and resurrection. None seemed to have been fully converted before Christ's crucifixion. One betrayed Him, and Peter cursed and swore that he didn't know Jesus (Matt. 26:47, 48; 69-75).

The twelve constantly disputed among themselves about "which one of them was the greatest" (Luke 22:14-27). They were still hung up on the same topic when they and Christ trod the path to Gethsemane (Matt. 20:17-28). Yet, even with all these seeming failures, they were the very ones Christ summoned to be the leaders of His church.

Then Christ went to the grave and His mission appeared to have failed for sure. His so-called "chosen" had run and Christ was dead and buried in a tomb. When we look at the total picture up to this point, judging it simply by what meets the human eye, His mission appeared a total and complete flop. If we valued Christ's ministry by typical human standards, Jesus failed big time! Had I been Jesus and had to work with the same congregation He had, I probably would have folded up my sermon notes and turned in my ministerial credentials!

Let's face it, we all like success! We like to see it, smell it, savor it, grasp it, touch it, and (if you are a minister), best of all, count it and report it to the conference office!

I remember the time I attended a ministerial meeting at which the yearly baptismal report was handed out. It showed how many baptisms each pastor had reported up to that time of the year. The document listed more than 30 pastors, and I had the only big fat zero! Then, as if that weren't bad enough, one of the conference officials said, "If David Farmer will have a baptism before the end of the year, it will be the first time in the history of this conference that every pastor will have had a baptism during the year." I could have died. Talk about embarrassment and feeling like a total failure! That had to have been the most mortifying moment of my life.

I know that the conference official did not mean it the way it sounded, but still, I was hurt and embarrassed. Before the year was up, though, I did have a baptism—in fact, three. And I give God all the credit. But nevertheless, at that meeting I felt like a complete loser—and I did not like appearing as a failure! No one does. Over time, however, I have learned that apparent failure and ultimate failure are not the same thing, as in my stories of the three evangelistic meetings that seemed to have failed but had been successful all along. I just didn't know it at the time. My success came to view later.

I planted the seeds that had to germinate underground, where I could not see them. My problem is I want to cultivate and harvest in three or four weeks. Most evangelists do. Many of us cannot tolerate failure or even any delay that appears to be failure. We like immediate success! Just as we want our prayers to be answered—immediately! And when they are not, or it appears they are not, then we feel as if we have failed at even knowing how to pray, too.

But again, look at Christ. He planted seeds with His disciples and the fruit wasn't seen fully until after Pentecost. By then He was in heaven. "Men sow the seed from which, above their graves, others reap blessed harvests. They plant trees, that others may eat the fruit. They are content here to know that they have set in motion agencies for good. In the hereafter the action and reaction of all these will be seen" (*Education,* p. 306).

As Christians, we must come to understand that what appears to be a lack of success in witnessing is not real failure. Do you realize this is one of the main reasons many Christians never witness for God? They are afraid of failing, believing that failure means they are losers. And losers never get trusted with any important assignments! So they feel that they are better off not doing anything. That way they can never fail. The sanguine and melancholic temperaments are probably the weakest in this area. But we all need to understand that anyone can succeed at doing nothing at all. It's much easier and much less threatening simply to sit in a comfortable pew and criticize others for the job they're doing.

Often as a church we try new projects and new programs. Some seem to work; others do not. I hate it when a new program comes out and gets promoted as something that will work for every member. Many try it, and if it doesn't succeed for them, they feel as if they have again failed God. Wouldn't it be better if all programs were designed with a person's temperament in mind?

We should never fear failing when it comes to witnessing for Jesus. But we should be afraid of not being willing to take a risk. It is only those who quit trying that we can consider failures. Thomas Edison tried hundreds of times before inventing the right filament that would work in a lightbulb. Abe Lincoln and Winston Churchill both lost several elections before entering their place in history. I have heard that it was on the 409th try that the household cleaner Formula 409 was invented. We must realize that only those who are doing something have the opportunity to appear to fail—or better yet, succeed!

We need to look beyond the discouragement and problems that we find in the church and our daily lives. Each of us must put behind us our past witnessing and see what roads God has for us to travel today. I heard a quote once that went something like this: "If you fail to plan, then you are planning to fail." Ellen White said that "as the people are anxious to hear, and many embrace the truth, *the gift which God has given His servants is called out and strengthened. They see that their efforts are crowned with success*" (*Testimonies for the Church,* vol. 1, p. 147; italics supplied). *"We fail many times because we do not realize that Christ is with us* by His Spirit as truly as when, in the days of His humiliation, He moved visibly upon the earth. The lapse of time has wrought no change in His parting promise to His apostles as He was taken up from them into heaven: 'Lo, I am with you alway, even unto the end of the world'" (*ibid.,* vol. 4, p. 529; italics supplied).

It doesn't matter what our temperaments are or what our past witnessing record shows. We can make a comeback in witnessing if we will only allow the Holy Spirit to lead us. Take the gift that God has given us and use it to His glory. His promise is "Lo, I am with you alway, even unto the end of the world" (Matt. 28:20). Believe it and find the witnessing program that fits your needs, then bounce back. You can do it!

Chapter 8

Gone Fishing

GO YE into all the world, and preach the gospel to every creature' (Mark 16:15), is Christ's command to His followers. Not that all are called to be ministers or missionaries in the ordinary sense of the term; *but all may be workers with Him in giving the 'glad tidings' to their fellow men.* To all, great or small, learned or ignorant, old or young, the command is given" (*Education,* p. 264; italics supplied).

Many years ago I watched a movie on television that starred Rock Hudson and Doris Day. Hudson portrayed a world-class fisherman who always had the answers when it came to questions about fishing. He even had written a book on the subject. Throughout the beginning of the movie fishermen would line up and ask Hudson questions about fishing, and he would tell them where the best place to fish was that day, what kind of fish were biting, the best bait to use, and how deep to fish. The lead character had answers to anything they wanted to know.

There was only one problem: Rock Hudson had never gone fishing in his life, but no one knew it. Then something happened. Someone asked him to be in a fishing tournament, and that's when the truth came out. Not once in his entire life had he placed a hook in the water.

Hudson could answer questions only because he listened to the fishermen who shopped at the sporting goods store where he worked. They would talk about their fishing experience for that day, and then Hudson would pass on that same information to others as the latest gospel about fishing. He was a good listener, but not a good fisherman.

That movie reminded me of a time my father took me fishing with him. The fish were not biting at all that day. I just sat there in the hot sun with my line in the water, checking it every few minutes or so. My father was on the other side of the creek, and I watched him as he kept changing his lures. He would try one for a few minutes, then another if he didn't get any strikes. But if he had a strike on a certain lure, Dad would continue to cast in the same spot with the same lure until the fish took the bait.

Often Dad would try to give me some advice on how to catch fish and what lure they were biting on, but I wouldn't listen. A die-hard worm fan, I liked using my trusted old worms for bait. "If the fish were biting, then worms would do the trick" was my motto. Needless to say, I didn't catch a thing that day, but my father caught his limit.

Years later my cousin Steve, an accomplished fisherman, took me out fishing with him. He has that natural ability to know the spots were the fish hide and seems always to know what bait or lure to use and when. The first time I went out with him, he taught me how to cast and hit a spot within two feet of my target. Because I listened to him that day, I learned a lot about casting.

Steve started catching fish right away. But even though I had listened earlier to what he had to say, I wasn't pulling a thing except a log or two. I couldn't figure out why. Then

Steve said something to me that still sticks in my memory: "The fish may not like your smell."

"What?" I asked in rather a loud voice. "I had a bath this morning and do not stink. Besides, how could the fish smell me when I'm on the bank and they're under water?"

He said that I didn't understand. What he meant was that the fish could smell my scent on the bait. He explained that when I baited the hook or picked up a lure, the odor from my fingers would rub off on it. And I might be one of those unfortunate individuals who stink to fish. I thought he had gone nuts and didn't mind telling him so in a Christian sort of way. Then he asked if I would like him to prove it. Finally I agreed to his moronic idea just so I could make him look like a fool. Baiting my hook, he told me to cast it in the same spot I had been fishing. A few minutes later I caught a fish. It wasn't a record-breaking specimen, but it was a fish. So I asked Steve to bait my hook again, and sure enough, I caught another.

To this day I like to ask others to bait my hook if I'm not catching anything, or I try to wear gloves. It doesn't matter how many times I wash my hands; the fish still do not like my scent. I guess Steve was right—I "stink to fish"!

Are we ever like that in our witnessing? Do we witness is such a way that we "stink to people"? I'm afraid we sometimes do. We think that people should understand that what we say is the truth and that they had better accept it. And when they don't, we depart in such a way that we leave them with a bad taste in their mouth.

A choleric pastor friend of mine was at a flea market, wandering from booth to booth. At one of them he came upon a man wearing a Masonic ring. Without batting an eye, the pastor asked him if he knew how the Masons came about and that they were of the devil. The man gave the pastor a look that would burn a hole right through you, turned, and walked away.

When the pastor told the incident to me, I could tell that he was quite proud of himself for witnessing for the Lord. Probably he felt as if the recording angel had placed another check mark by his name for being a good and faithful servant. I asked him if he had ever won anyone to Christ with such forceful and straight questions before. After thinking about it for what seemed to be a long time, he finally said no. At least he was being honest with me.

Was Christ ever overbearing with His questions? Not to my knowledge. He always approached others in such a way that they knew He understood their deepest feelings. Remember when Jesus asked Peter three times if he loved Him? (See the chapter "Back From Failure" and John 21:15-17.) Jesus wasn't being aggressive with His questions, but He did want to get His point across. And it took Peter a while to understand just what Christ had in mind. Finally he discerned that Christ wanted him to know that his service to others must be motivated by unconditional love.

Peter (who I believe must have been a sanguine, because almost every time you read about him in the Bible he is talking) must have been driven by something other than love in his approach to others. Because sanguines are naturally selfish, forward, and impulsive, Peter, who once was a boasting disciple, was now a changed man. "Three times Peter had openly denied his Lord, and three times Jesus drew from him the assurance of his love and loyalty, pressing home that pointed question, like a barbed arrow to his wounded heart. . . . Before his fall, Peter was always speaking unadvisedly, from the impulse of the moment. He was always ready to correct others, and to express his mind, before he had a clear comprehension of himself or of what he had to say. But the converted Peter was very different" (*The Desire of Ages,* p. 812).

Peter wasn't impatient, impetuous, self-confident, and self-exalted any longer. Now he was teachable and calm, ready to feed the flock of Christ. Having listened to his Saviour, he was now a "fisher of men" and ready to love others with an unconditional love.

Ellen White refers to the unconditional love we are to have for others today. She says that "the children of God are those who are partakers of His nature. It is not earthly rank, nor birth, nor nationality, nor religious privilege, which proves that we are members of the family of God; it is love, a love that embraces all humanity. . . . To be kind to the unthankful and to the evil, to do good hoping for nothing again, is the insignia of the royalty of heaven, the sure token by which the children of the Highest reveal their high estate" (*Thoughts From the Mount of Blessing,* p. 75).

Peter was a professional fisher as long as he was on the water, but he really knew nothing about fishing for people on dry land. Frog hunting is the reverse. Frogs are easy to catch on dry land, but it's different in water. They're at home there, can swim fast, and you have to have some knowledge of how to catch them. It's the same with catching fish. To be successful, you need some knowledge of when and where to fish. Oh sure, you will hear stories of those who had beginner's luck, but how much better would their success have been if they'd had a little training on how to catch fish. The same applies to fishing for human beings. How much more successful we could be if we studied using the right tools that God has given us.

Are we ever like Peter? Fishing without any knowledge of how to fish? Jesus once called His disciples and said, "Follow me, and *I will make* you fishers of men" (Matt. 4:19). He called, trained, and fashioned them into the kind of witnesses they needed to be. They were not to go fishing (witnessing) until *after* Jesus had given them some training. Our Saviour wanted them to know who He was and what His mission was all about. If they had no knowledge of who He was, who had sent Him, and what His purpose was, how could they tell others?

"To have the higher education is to have a living connection with Christ. The Saviour took the unlearned fishermen from their boats and their fishing nets and connected them with Himself as He traveled from place to place, teaching the people and ministering to their needs. . . . There are many men and women who suppose that they know all that is worth knowing, when they greatly need to sit humbly at the feet of Jesus and learn of Him who gave His life that He might redeem a fallen world" (*Testimonies for the Church,* vol. 9, p. 174).

I remember the time I first felt the call to become a literature evangelist. It was 1980 in a small eastern Texas town, and I had been back in the church for a little more than a year and was working as a diesel mechanic helper and truck driver. I enjoyed my job but wanted to do more for the Lord. When our local literature evangelist heard that I desired to do something for God, he went to work on me. In fact, he was trying to persuade two others at the same time that selling Christian books was the best employment a person could have. And he did a pretty good job at convincing all three of us, because we all decided at the same time to join him in selling Christian books.

The next Sabbath after the colporteur talked to me, I prayed and asked God to give me a sign if He was calling me. I wanted to know for sure, although I really didn't have a doubt. The sign I asked for was to let me have a flat tire on the way to work Monday morning.

Come Monday morning, I left the house, walked around my car, and guess what? No flat. I thought, *That's OK, Lord; just give me one on the way to work.* We lived about five miles away, so He had plenty of time. Every mile, every second, I kept waiting. As I got closer to work and still had no flat, I thought that God was testing me to see if I would doubt Him. But when I drove into the parking lot, my heart sank. God wasn't calling me as I just knew He was. My whole day was shot. I walked around dragging my feet and looking as if one of our big Mack diesel trucks had run over me.

By the next morning, being the sanguine I am, I had forgotten about it. I got up as usual, hopped into my VW, and headed down the road toward work. About halfway I had a flat. On my best tire, yet. It left me a little perplexed and confused. Had God misconstrued my prayer? Had He been so busy the day before that He couldn't get around to answering until now?

The incident baffled me all that day. I prayed and asked God to let me know what was going on. I had not revealed my first prayer to anyone. It was a silent request between Him and me. I do not make a habit out of asking God for signs, so I was sure it wasn't the devil playing tricks on me.

But what was God telling me? After much prayer, I believe God impressed me with what He was doing.

If I had had the flat the day before, when I had asked for it, I would have marched right into my boss's office and informed him that I was giving him a two-week notice. In fact, I had already planned my speech and knew exactly what I was going to say. But since the flat came a day later, I hadn't said anything.

After I spent much time in prayer, the answer came. God impressed me that I had never read any of the books I was about to sell. How could I sell something that I really didn't know, understand, or even accept and believe? So that evening I started reading *The Desire of Ages.* Since then I have read through it twice more. It has become one of my all-time favorite books, and Ellen White is by far my favorite author.

After finishing *The Desire of Ages,* I read *The Great Controversy,* then *Patriarchs and Prophets.* At this time I felt the call again from God. Finally He opened the door for me, and I became a literature evangelist. I still remember Ellen White's observation that "to the unlearned, toiling fishermen of Galilee was the call addressed: 'Follow me, and I will make you fishers of men' (Matt. 4:19). These disciples were humble and teachable. The less they had been influenced by the false teaching of their time, the more successfully could Christ instruct and train them for His service. . . . *It is God's plan to employ humble instruments to accomplish great results.* Then the glory will not be given to men, but to Him who works through them to will and to do of His own good pleasure" (*The Great Controversy,* p. 171; italics supplied).

Today I am convinced God has called every true believer into His service. "God wants every individual in His service to represent Him" (*General Conference Bulletin*, Apr. 3, 1901). Telling others of the coming Messiah, we are to travel down rugged and dusty roads. But not until He has trained us. I'm not talking about formal training, but knowing who Christ is. To know Him as your personal Saviour. To have faith in who He is and not to be concerned about failing. If Jesus has trained us and sends us into the world, we have nothing to be ashamed of. Nothing to worry about. "Those who will obey the words of inspiration, 'Go work today in my vineyard,' *who will study how they can cooperate with Christ* in causing the light of truth to shine to those nigh and to those afar off in the darkness of error, *will receive special aid from God*. But this work can not be done without self-denial and self-sacrifice. . . . The members of His church are to be laborers together with Him; and as they work for others, God will impress minds and hearts. Let both men and women engage with their whole hearts in this missionary work, and holiness to God will be the result. *All who will train themselves for the Master's service may obtain a rich, golden experience*" (*Review and Herald*, Nov. 14, 1899; italics supplied).

If we hate one thing when it comes to fishing, it is coming home empty-handed. Almost without fail, when we walk through the door our mates meet us and ask the dreaded question: "Did you catch anything?" As if the whole fishing trip is based on how many fish we catch. But fishing is far more than just catching fish. There is the sport, the outdoors, the fellowship with other fishers. Catching the fish is just the extra bonus that comes with the sport.

We don't always have to return home with the trophy to be successful fishers.

It's the same with witnessing for God. We do not always have to come home with great news about how many we brought to Christ today or how many Bible studies we have given to be considered successful. I remember leaving Bible studies many times with tears in my eyes. Also, I have been with many other sincere individuals who wept for someone who had turned a deaf ear to them. But it shouldn't stop us from witnessing.

That's like saying "I tried fishing once and didn't catch anything, so I'll never try it again." Most fishers, if they are honest, will tell you that on the vast majority of their fishing trips they catch nothing or very little.

I believe that some of our conferences make a big mistake when they base the success of a pastor or evangelist on how many baptisms they have had for that year. I don't care how good a fisher you are, if you fish in places where there aren't any fish or the fish are not biting, you will not catch anything. The same rule applies for soul winning. If you witness in an area in which the people are not interested in hearing our message, then you will have fewer Bible studies and baptisms.

Doesn't Jesus tell us in Matthew 10:14 that "whosoever shall not receive you, nor hear your words, when ye depart out of that *house* or *city,* shake off the dust of your feet"? There will be cities, streets, countries (see Luke 8:37), and homes that will not welcome the good news. But then on the other hand, whole cities might accept the message as did Nineveh (Jonah 3:5-10) and the region of Decapolis that welcomed Jesus back in Luke 8:40.

I remember another fishing trip with my two sons and father at a rather large pond in central Texas. As we stood on the bank, we used minnows with two hooks on each line. It was a fishing dream-come-true trip. Every time we cast our line, the moment it hit the water, *bam!* two bass would hit. I've never seen anything like it before or since. We threw back those that weighed less than a pound. I remember remarking to my father, "Boy, I wish we had a boat!"

"But son, we can't pull them in any faster!" he replied. (Sometimes we are never satisfied and want still more.)

I believe there will come a time when our "fishing for men" will be like that. We will have those to whom we have witnessed coming in faster than we can "pull them in." At the time I wrote this chapter the General Conference reported that five new Seventh-day Adventist churches were being erected every 24 hours and more than 1,800 baptisms a day were taking place worldwide.

If you are a fisher, then I'm sure you have experienced times when you caught a nice-sized fish and everyone around you started casting their line toward the same spot. (Aggravating, isn't it?) Have you noticed that other religions do the exact same thing? When we traveled to Russia the second time, many different denominations were there telling about the love of Christ. Many had done an excellent job of witnessing, but some had done damage.

One charismatic evangelist in the city we visited had preached nothing but that the people should give him their money and God would bless them. He left a lot of people with a bad taste in their mouth about Christianity. His witnessing had done great harm. We must watch how we witness for the Lord. Ellen White declares that "there are souls perplexed with doubt, burdened with infirmities, weak in faith, and unable to grasp the Unseen; but a friend whom they can see, coming to them in Christ's stead, can be a connecting link to fasten their trembling faith upon Christ" (*The Desire of Ages,* p. 297).

The fact that Satan has his "witnesses" out there among God's flock is one reason we must be ready and willing to go wherever God sends us. Many will not go to foreign lands, but will instead have their mission field in their own backyard. God may use others to advance His cause by providing financial support for others. Whatever God summons you to, do it with all your might. Always remember whom you are working for.

Fishing for human beings does not take a lot of training and is not a great art that only a few can do. "He who called the fishermen of Galilee is still calling men and women to His service. And He is just as willing to manifest His power through us as through the first disciples. However imperfect and sinful we may be, the Lord holds out to us the offer of partnership with Himself, of apprenticeship to Christ. He invites us to come under the divine instruction, that, uniting with Christ, we may work the works of God" (*ibid.*). "'Go ye into all the world, and preach the gospel to every creature' (Mark 16:15). These are the Lord's commands. Are the great body of professed Christians doing this work?" (*Christ's Object Lessons,* p. 371).

Since we are all called to fish (witness), and it is Christ who teaches us, then shouldn't we want to fish (witness) the best way we know how? Just as all fishers use their skills and knowledge, we should witness with our skills and knowledge. Fishers know their gear, the right spots to fish, and which bait or lure to use. They spend time at the sporting goods store reading and studying each new item. Should we not do the same? "It is a great thing to believe on Jesus Christ. We have altogether too little faith. . . . The Master has given to every man his work. And because others may not do just exactly the work you have to do, do not feel that you must criticize everything they do. No, indeed! No one ought to devote to faultfinding the time that he ought to spend in *hunting for souls, fishing for souls, using every capability and power in his appointed work.* When your powers are used in this way, you may know that the Lord God of heaven is right by your side, to strengthen and to guide" (*Spalding and Magan's Unpublished Manuscript Testimonies of Ellen G. White,* p. 372; italics supplied).

Chapter 9

Down-to-earth Witnessing the Wrong Way

LET NONE be impatient and angry when friends set before them the errors, mistakes, and dangers of the course they have been taking. So long have they cherished their own ways, that they have become self-confident, and do not discern that they have serious defects of character which exert an influence over those with whom they are brought in contact. They do not *realize that their influence* will cause others to cherish a wrong spirit, to rise up against order and discipline, to disregard the wishes of those who have the *rule over them,* and who watch over their souls as they that must give an account. Shall those who are cherishing serious defects of character, and sowing their evil seeds in the souls of others, continue in this course of action? Let us read what the apostle has written in the word of God: 'Do all things without murmurings and disputings.' How much murmuring and disputing is indulged in by those who are counseled and reproved! They dispute with the one who labors for their good. *They refuse to believe that their influence is anything but good and praiseworthy"* (*Youth's Instructor,* Aug. 24, 1893; italics supplied).

When I came back into the church in the early part of 1979, I heard a lot of talk about receiving the latter rain. I remember meeting at the pastor's home one Sabbath afternoon with some other men from the church. We lived in a small city about 20 miles away from the pastor, and I rode over with another man who had some different ideas than the traditional Seventh-day Adventist might have. He was a good man, meant well, and was sincere, but also, I believe, sincerely wrong in his beliefs.

Because he had brought up many of his theories and ideas at church and other places, the pastor decided to confront him that Sabbath afternoon. Needless to say, the man was hurt and embarrassed. But what impressed me, even though I still believe he was wrong on some of his theology, was that he acted like a Christian to the pastor and the other church members. The latter, sadly, were rather unchristian.

Lately I have discovered that witnessing can be done in one of two ways. We can either be one of God's faithful few or Satan's deceitful many. If you gave criminals a surgeon's knife, they would likely use it totally differently than the manufacturer intended. It's the person, not the tool, that determines the outcome.

The same rule can apply to Christian witnessing. Ellen White declares that "he who would confess Christ must have Christ abiding in him. He cannot communicate that which he has not received" (*The Desire of Ages,* p. 357). If we do not have Christ in our hearts, then how can we ever expect to share Him with others?

You've heard the saying "Guns don't kill people; people kill people." Let's reword that to say "Religion doesn't kill people; people kill religion." When we do not have Christ in our hearts before we witness to others about Him, it is as if we "kill religion." "Frivolity, selfish indulgence, and careless indifference on the part of professed Christians are *turning away many souls* from the path of life" (*Christ's Object Lessons*, p. 341; italics supplied). "How many prodigals are kept out of the kingdom of God *by the unlovely character of those who claim to be Christians.* Jealousy, envy, pride, and uncharitable feelings, self-righteousness easily provoked, thinking evil, harshness, coldness, lack of sympathy, these are the attributes of Satan. . . . The worker has in many instances developed similar attributes which have marred the soul of the one with whom he is dealing" (*Spalding and Magan's Unpublished Manuscript Testimonies of Ellen G. White,* p. 144; italics supplied).

Have you ever wondered why it seems that the church is not reaching as many people in America as it does in other countries? I wanted to see what Ellen White commented on the subject. And if you are like me, you may not like what she has to say about witnessing the wrong way. *"Unconverted church members may do the same things that Christians do, with altogether a different spirit and different motives.* The words and acts of a Christian are a savor of life unto life; the words and acts of a hypocritical church member are a savor of death unto death" (*Review and Herald,* 1903; italics supplied). "If we would humble ourselves before God, and be kind and courteous and tenderhearted and pitiful, there would be one hundred conversions to the truth where now there is only one" (*Testimonies for the Church,* vol. 9, p. 189).

When I first read all that she had to say about unconverted church members, I wondered what it had to do with soul winning. But then I concluded—a lot! I guess it all depends on your perspective on the matter. Your point of view on witnessing for Jesus.

Perhaps you remember seeing the Amazing Facts brochure depicting a tall hat. The caption beneath the illustration asks, "Is the distance from the top of the hat to the bottom or the distance across the brim greater?" When you first glance at the hat, you just know that it is much taller than it is wide. But it is actually wider than tall. Because your eyes disagreed, you want to take out a ruler and measure it for yourself. To your surprise, you discover that the caption is correct. I guess it is how you view the matter, your perspective. And even then, it is still difficult to believe.

Someone once said, "I thought I was poor because I had no shoes, until I met a man who had no feet." Perspective. It all depends on your point of view, doesn't it?

Once I visited a small village in Mexico. It contained only a couple dozen homes, and up to 10 or more family members lived in each small dwelling. Many of the mud huts had outdoor toilets behind them. Unwashed kids ran up to us, trying to sell rocks they had found lying around or to beg for money. As I stood there looking at the kids, it dawned on me how rich I must appear to them. I had on new clothes, nice shoes, and had had a bath and a haircut recently. Then I thought of my three-bedroom, two-bath house with a yard back home. Suddenly I felt the wealth of a king.

Then a few years later, working as a literature evangelist, I received a card from a house far out in the county. It took me more than an hour to locate the place. When I finally found the mailbox with the person's name and address on it, I had to go through two huge gates and continue up a small blacktop road. As I rounded the first curve, I saw the most immense mansion you could image. A dozen or so columns held up the front entrance, and it looked like something you would see movie stars living in on television. Instantly I felt extremely poor. Again, I guess it is how you view the matter, what your perspective might be. What may appear as rich to some may be poor to another. A person can view one thing one way, and another individual can see the same thing as something entirely different.

I believe the same principle can apply to witnessing. You witness for good or you witness for evil—it's all how you view the matter, your perspective toward witnessing.

During the past several years I have identified three kinds of people involved in witnessing: those who witness in their own temperament, those who expect everyone to witness the way they do, and those who don't care how you witness or if you witness at all.

Those who want to control the way others witness often seek to run the show and have the final say on what people present and how they testify for Jesus. They believe theirs is the only way because it works for them. John had to deal with such a person in his Third Epistle. The disciple was writing to a congregation dominated by a strong, one-sided, almost dictatorial type by the name of Diotrephes. Diotrephes assumed the power to cast others from the church, possibly by a form of excommunication or disfellowship. It may be that he was the elder of the church and that he had accepted some of the false teachings of the Gnostics. Commenting on the passage, *The Seventh-day Adventist Bible Commentary* concludes that "the basic heresy against which John is contending has been identified as a sort of proto-Gnosticism, which taught false *gnōsis,* that is, false knowledge. . . . Docetism denied the reality of the incarnation and taught that Christ only *appeared* to have a human body. . . . The originators and supporters of these heresies are graphically described by John as 'antichrists' . . . and 'false prophets.' . . . To combat these errors he stresses the reality of Christ's visible human nature during the incarnation . . . , that He did come in the flesh . . . , and that believers may enjoy this true knowledge . . . as opposed to the false *gnōsis"* (*The Seventh-day Adventist Bible Commentary,* vol. 7, pp. 625, 626).

When John wrote to the churches to rebuke such false teaching, Diotrephes appears to have refused to read the letter to the members (3 John 9). Visiting ministers possibly sent by John also could not get a hearing, and those who listened to them privately found themselves disfellowshiped by the arrogant Diotrephes. Harboring unholy ambition, he aspired to be first for the sake of position rather than for the sake of the good he might accomplish.

We should never allow this sort of apostasy in God's house. When we have leaders who want to dictate every move of God's church, we will have a problem. I had such an experience with a leader in a church that I attended many years ago. We had just elected church officers for the coming year. Most had accepted their position, but a few had declined, and the nominating committee would have to meet again. One church leader, not wanting to wait for the committee to convene again, demanded that we read the names on the Sabbath as if they had all accepted their office. His position caused a lot of disunity among many church members.

One of the newly elected elders who disagreed with the idea of the names being read had to be out of town that Sabbath. He asked me to read a letter he had written to the church before anyone presented the names to them. Being head elder at the time, I glanced at his letter and thought there should be no problem with reading it up front, since he was not going to be present. The letter basically said that he thought the report from the nominating committee should not be given as if everyone had accepted their positions when some had not.

That Sabbath I showed the letter to a certain church officer who then stood in my way and refused to allow me to read the letter. He saw no need for it. I told him as nicely as I could that I was going to present it. After much persuasion, he finally agreed to let me read the letter. As I started walking toward the pulpit, he darted in front of me and started with the nominating committee report before the pianist even stopped playing her song. Floored, I stood there not wanting to believe what was happening. When I had to mention that I was to read my letter first, he looked at the congregation and said, "Letter? What letter? David says he has some letter he wants to read. I know nothing about a letter to be read." Then he sat down.

It was more than I could handle. How a Christian could sit there and lie was beyond anything I could comprehend. The incident caused a serious split in the church—all because he wanted to run everything his way.

The Bible warns us and experience tells us that whenever someone dominates the work of God's church, problems will arise. I don't care if the person is the pastor, elder, deacon, deaconess, or whoever; God will not stand for it.

Ellen White counsels men and women with the desire to run God's church. *"How many churches have been divided,* making the cause of truth a byword and a reproach among the wicked! . . . The children of God the world over are one family, *and the same spirit of love and conciliation should govern them.* 'Be kindly affectioned one to another with brotherly love; in honor preferring one another' (Rom. 12:10), is the teaching of our Saviour. The cultivation of a uniform courtesy, a willingness to do to others as we would wish them to do to us, would annihilate half the ills of life. The spirit of self-aggrandizement is the spirit of Satan; but the heart in which the love of Christ is cherished, will possess that charity which seeketh not her own. Such will heed the divine injunction, 'Look not every man on his own things, but every man also on the things of others' (Phil. 2:4)" (*Patriarchs and Prophets,* p. 132; italics supplied).

Whether it be good or bad, our influence on others is strong. The church leader in my story above almost drove some members to quit coming to church altogether. Many members did leave that local congregation and started attending another one in a different town. I was one of them. His bad influence still disturbs many members. "Never should it be forgotten that influence is no less a power for evil. To lose one's own soul is a terrible thing; *but to cause the loss of other souls is still more terrible.* That our influence should be a savor of death unto death is a fearful thought; yet this is possible. Many who profess to gather with Christ are scattering from Him. This is why the church is so weak. Many indulge freely in criticism and accusing. By giving expression to suspicion, jealousy, and discontent, they yield themselves as instruments to Satan. Before they realize what they are doing, the adversary has through them accomplished his purpose. . . . Distrust, unbelief, and downright infidelity have fastened upon those who otherwise might have accepted Christ. Meanwhile the workers for Satan look complacently upon those whom they have driven to skepticism, and who are now hardened against reproof and entreaty. They flatter themselves that in comparison with these souls they are virtuous and righteous. They do not realize that these sad wrecks of character are the work of their own unbridled tongues and rebellious hearts. It is through their influence that these tempted ones have fallen" (*Christ's Object Lessons,* pp. 340, 341).

I have found that some church members can be highly critical of the way others witness. Let me give you an example. Regardless of what you or I think about celebration churches, they witness to a group that many of us may never reach. Celebration-style church members feel uncomfortable with traditional church services. They want to "celebrate" Christ in a way that many of us would find ourselves highly uneasy with. Is that wrong? It all depends on your "perspective" of it and whom you ask.

I once had a member in Iowa buy me a set of drums. One Sabbath afternoon several members wanted to get together and play some gospel music. Being from the South, I remarked that I like bluegrass-style gospel music. Then I mentioned that I used to be a drummer in a band but now I played only the guitar. After some discussion, we agreed to get together the next Sabbath evening and pick and sing some.

A young woman there had just recently starting coming back to church after being away for many years. She picked up on my statement that I had once been a drummer, so she bought her new pastor a used set of drums.

She had them covered when I arrived. After I walked in and talked a little, she and another couple who were soon to be members threw back the tarp and yelled, "Surprise!" And was I ever. My first thought was *What will the church members think?* And worse, *What will the conference officials say?* But after I looked over my new set of drums for a few minutes, we started playing some good southern gospel, and I have to say, I had a great time. Yes, drums and all.

Monday morning I called the conference secretary and told him the whole story. He asked me what I planned to do with the drums. "Just play them over at her house," I replied. "Then go have a good time and don't worry about it," he advised. Now, regardless of how you feel about drums, it is one of the avenues God used to win the woman, as well as a good friend of hers, her daughter, and her new husband. Today they are strong workers for the Lord in Iowa. On special occasions they go to nursing homes and play gospel music to the people there. (In case you don't know it, that is called witnessing for the Lord within your talent.)

Now, for those wondering whatever became of the drum set, I gave them back to the woman who had given them to me when I received an invitation to return to the Gulf States Conference. Explaining that not all members would understand their pastor having a set of drums at his home, I asked if she would sell them to regain some of her money. She didn't want to, but she did.

One time I related the incident to our union evangelist, and he advised me to get rid of the drums immediately. He considered them of the devil! But to this day I'm glad I listened to the Holy Spirit instead of him.

I cannot overemphasize the fact that witnessing can do a lot of good if done in its proper perspective. The absolute heart of witnessing is knowing when to speak and when to stay quiet. And when we do speak, it must always be done in a Christ-centered manner rather than in a way that brings terror to others. For example, not everyone is ready to hear about the mark of the beast. Most need to hear about Jesus first. If they have not heard the good news about Christ and His forgiveness, then knowing about the mark of the beast, the Sabbath, the state of the dead, etc., will do them no good.

We also need to know when a person is ready to receive a book we would like to give them. A newly baptized member gave her Catholic father *The Great Controversy* right after she joined the church. Her father read the whole book and demanded that his daughter quit the denomination. I tried talking to him about reading *The Desire of Ages, Christ's Object Lessons,* or *Steps to Christ,* but he wouldn't hear of it. He thought we were against Catholics.

On the other hand, I know of a case in which a doctor read *The Great Controversy* and is a church elder today. In fact, thousands of individuals have responded similarly. But the point is knowing what book to give and when to give it to those you are witnessing to. "Those who are seeking for truth need to have words *spoken to them in season;* for Satan is speaking to them by his temptations. If you meet with repulse when trying to help souls, heed it not. If there seems to be little good resulting from your work, do not become discouraged. Keep working; be discreet; *know when to speak, and when to keep silent;* watch for souls as they that must give an account; and watch for the devices of Satan, lest you be led aside from duty" (*Gospel Workers,* pp. 188, 189; italics supplied).

Whatever your perspective of witnessing is, always keep in mind that there is a proper way and an improper way: God's way and Satan's. "God's way is to make man something he is not; God's plan is to set man to work in reformatory lines; then he will learn by experience how long he has pampered fleshly appetites, and ministered to his own temperament, bringing weakness upon himself" (*Healthful Living,* p. 33).

Chapter 10

The Domino Effect

W HEN YOU carry this message to those in cities who are hungry for truth, and they accept the light, they will go earnestly to work to bring that light to others. *Souls who have means will bring others into the truth,* and will give of their means to advance the cause of God" (*Life Sketches,* p. 418; italics supplied).

I'm sure you have heard of, or perhaps even been involved in, one of the many multilevel network marketing plans. A person brings someone else into a sales plan, that individual recruits another, and on and on. Each person receives a percentage of the sales of the new people. If enough people get recruited, those who started the plan could theoretically become millionaires. I have tried my hand at such a money-making formula a time or two, and so far have made the grand total of $0.00.

In fact, I have yet to meet anyone who has made any *real* money to speak of. But would such a plan work for God's church? Would it be successful then? If we looked at this method in terms of everyone having hundreds of baptisms, probably not. But how many baptisms does a person have to have to be considered successful? Listen to what Ellen White says she saw in vision: "We all entered the cloud together, and were seven days ascending to the sea of glass, when Jesus brought along the crowns and with His own right hand placed them on our heads. He gave us harps of gold and palms of victory. Here on the sea of glass the 144,000 stood in a perfect square. Some of them had very bright crowns, others not so bright. Some crowns appeared heavy with stars, while others had but few. *All were perfectly satisfied with their crowns"* (*A Word to the Little Flock,* p. 15; italics supplied).

From what I understand her statement to mean, numbers don't count in heaven. The only thing that does is whether we did the witnessing God gave us the ability to do. Paul states in 1 Corinthians 12:28-31: "And God hath set some in the church, first apostles, secondarily prophets, thirdly teachers, after that miracles, then gifts of healings, helps, governments, diversities of tongues. Are all apostles? are all prophets? are all teachers? are all workers of miracles? Have all the gifts of healing? do all speak with tongues? do all interpret? But covet earnestly the best gifts."

Not everyone can have the success of Mark Finley, H.M.S. Richards, Sr., or Kenneth Cox. God doesn't expect us to. To the vast majority, God sends only a few people for us to witness to. I remember someone telling me that Ron Halvorsen, Sr., was the only person baptized as a result of the evangelistic series he attended. But look at how many he has brought to Christ. And of the ones he has helped save, only God knows how many others they have brought to God.

I recently attended an evangelism council in Daytona Beach, Florida. While there I ran across an evangelist by the name of Dick Pollard, who baptized me when I was 12 years old. It was nice going up and asking him if he recalled conducting a series in a bubble tent in Odessa, Texas, in 1966. When he said yes, I then asked him if he remembered baptizing a small boy along with the others. Looking at me, he asked, "Was that you?" We had fun reminiscing, and he inquired about the members in Odessa. Also, he was happy to know that one of his converts had become a pastor.

When we were in Russia the second time, we had four young Seventh-day Adventist girls helping each night at the meetings. They told us how they had come into the church. It seems that one of the girls had become an Adventist because of a friend. She then told one of her friends, who told one of her friends, who told one of her friends, and the list just kept on going. I have no way of knowing how many friends and family members joined God's church from their witnessing.

Before we left Russia, we traveled back to the city where we had been the year before. We wanted to see all the friends we had made and find out how the church was doing. One of the members I had baptized the year before invited us over to her home for lunch. As we sat there eating, her husband told us the following story.

His wife could neither read nor write. And because she was not able to read the Bible we had given her the year before, she had asked him, a Communist atheist, to read it to her. Listening to him talk, it was obvious that he was a highly intelligent man. He told us that he had served as a Communist leader for years. Although he hated religion and anything that had to do with God, he loved his wife, so he read to her nightly the story of Jesus and His love, His forgiveness, and His promise to return soon. Before long he fell in love with the One he had despised just a few months before.

Today he is the head deacon, in charge of building their new church sanctuary. As we sat there eating and listening to his remarkable story, he said to me, "Isn't it great that two families from the two most powerful countries in the world, countries that have hated each other for years, can now sit down and eat from the same table in the name of Christ?" All I could say was "Amen!"

But isn't that what being a Christian is all about? Being able to sit down with your "enemies" in the name of Christ and eat together. As Christians, we should be color-blind and love our enemies. The color of a person's skin or the country they come from should have nothing to do with our witnessing to them. God loves us all and commands us to do the same. "Beloved, if God so loved us, we ought also to love one another" (1 John 4:11). Nowhere does God say we are to love just a certain race or class of people. We are to assist Christ in winning everyone He leads to us and then help train them to become disciples themselves. "Go ye therefore, and teach all nations, baptizing them in the name of the Father, and of the Son, and of the Holy Ghost: teaching them to observe all things whatsoever I have commanded you: and, lo, I am with you alway, even unto the end of the world" (Matt. 28:19, 20).

"The faithful sower of the seed will hear the commendation of the Master, 'Well done, thou good and faithful servant, . . . enter thou into the joy of the Lord.' What is the joy of our Lord? It is the joy of seeing souls for whom Christ died redeemed in the kingdom of glory. Those who enter into the joys of their Lord will have the blessed satisfaction of seeing souls saved in the mansions of God through *their instrumentality*. These souls will be as stars in the crown of their rejoicing" (*Review and Herald,* Jan. 2, 1879; italics supplied).

Paul urges us in 1 Corinthians 11:1 to "imitate me, . . . just as I imitate Christ" (TEV). It is the perfect example of what Christ wants us all to do—imitate Him. In other words, we should act like Him (be kind to others), dress like Him (modestly), speak like Him (pure words). But all too often we have our petty little squabbles that disrupt the progress of God's work. Such differences slow down everything, especially our witnessing programs. This is not God's way, nor are we imitating Christ. "Christ is the example, the standard. If you fail to imitate Christ, your influence leads others to do the same" (*Testimonies for the Church at Battle Creek,* p. 7).

What is especially sad is that I often find that our influence, whether good or bad, has a way of going ahead of us. "Throw a pebble into the lake, and a wave is formed, and another and another; and as they increase, the circle widens, until it reaches the very shore. So with our influence. Beyond our knowledge or control it tells upon others in blessing or in cursing" (*Christ's Object Lessons,* p. 340).

For years, whenever I would visit another church, I would often hear the same complaint from different members: "Our pastor never stops to visit in our home." That bothered me for years. Why didn't pastors visit more? Then I became a pastor. How I wish at times that I could clone myself. There just never seem to be enough hours in the day. Then I encountered something that really helped me.

"If the pastor never stops at your home, you probably should thank God. It means death has not struck, that no serious illness has laid you low, or that the surgeon's knife had not been necessary, or that you have had no serious family problem or that you are not a spiritually delinquent member. As a rule, your pastor does not have time for 'social calls.' It is not that he would not enjoy doing so, it is simply a matter of priories . . . putting first things first. Your pastor does not have time to do everything he would like to do. However, you may be sure of this: your pastor is willing to come to the hospital or your home, the jail, the street corner, or anywhere at any hour of the day or night when he is needed. Call him if you need him. Otherwise he will not know of your need until it is too late. For the moment, thank God you have not needed him. One day you will need him and he will be there when you call. Now he is visiting someone else who does need him" (Taken from the *Shepherdess International Journal,* Fourth Quarter 1995).

"There was an important job to be done and Everybody was sure that Somebody would do it. Anybody could have done it, but Nobody did it. Somebody got angry about that, because it was Everybody's job. Everybody thought Anybody could do it, but Nobody realized that Everybody blamed Somebody when Nobody did what Anybody could have."

A tongue twister for sure, but look at the truth in it. Constantly we allow others to do what God has asked us to do. We need to learn "the importance of personal effort, of making direct appeals to our kindred, friends, and neighbors. There are those who for a lifetime have professed to be acquainted with Christ, yet who have never made a personal effort to bring even one soul to the Saviour. They leave all the work for the minister. *He may be well qualified for his calling, but he cannot do that which God has left for the members of the church*" (*The Desire of Ages,* p. 141; italics supplied).

A friend wrote me about her 10-month-old grandchild who was just learning to walk. She said he would get up, take two steps forward, then four steps backward and fall. We are like that. We make a little progress in witnessing, take a few steps, then stumble back four steps and drop. But we need to do what my friend said her grandchild did next—get up and try again.

When I studied for a doctorate in Christian counseling, a lot of my coursework involved understanding the dynamics of our complex mind. I long to help others recognize how to work with what they have and what they are using as biblical principles. And I want everyone to know that God can use them to finish His work.

Let me give you an example, the story of a newly hired traveling salesman who sent his first sales report to the home office. It stunned the sales department, for here's what he had written: "I seen this outfit which ain't never bought a dimes worth of nothing from us & I sole them a cuple hundred thousand dollars of guds. I am now going to Chcawgo."

But before the sales manager could fire the illiterate salesman, he received another letter: "I cum hear un sole them haff a millyon."

Fearful if he did and fearful if he didn't fire the illiterate peddler, the sales manager decided to dump the problem in the lap of the president. The following morning everybody was flabbergasted to see the two letters posted on the bulletin board along with a memo from *the president* tacked above them: "We ben spending two much time trying to spel instid of trying to sel. Let wach those sails. I want everybody should read these liters from Gooch who is on the rode doin a grate job for us, un you shud go out and do lake he done."

Many Christians never witness or take part in a program for fear they are not capable. It is true that we ought to be our best for God, but it is also surely true that God can use whatever we have. Christ's disciples were not highly educated. "When they saw the boldness of Peter and John, and perceived that they were unlearned and ignorant men, they marvelled; and they took knowledge of them, that they had been with Jesus" (Acts 4:13).

Ellen White says that the unlearned and uneducated will have a major role in completing God's mission on earth. "Even though a church may be composed of poor and uneducated and unknown persons, yet if they are believing, praying members, their influence will be felt for time and for eternity. If they go forth in simple faith, relying upon the promises of the word of God, they may accomplish great good. . . . The poor, the unlearned, if they choose, may become students in the school of Christ, and he will teach them true wisdom. . . . Persons who are highly educated are likely to depend more upon their book knowledge than upon God" (*Review and Herald,* June 25, 1895). "Look for the conversion of a large number from the highways and the byways. *Unexpected talent will be developed in those in the common walks of life.* If men and women can have the message of truth brought to them, many who hear will receive it. Some who are *regarded as uneducated* will be called to the service of the Master, even as the humble, unlearned fishermen were called by the Saviour. Men will be called from the plow as was Elisha, and will take up the work that God has appointed them. They will begin to labor in simplicity and quietness, reading and explaining the Scriptures to others. *Their simple efforts will be successful"*

(*Review and Herald*, June 27, 1912; italics supplied).

Laity, not the pastors, will finish God's work. There just are not enough pastors to do what needs to done. When our church started keeping official statistics during the late 1800s it had about one pastor per 130 members. In the past decade the ratio has risen from 463 to 719 members per pastor (see Stanley A. Hudson, "Pastoral Roles in Adventism's First Century," *Ministry*, June 1997). With those statistics worsening daily, you can see why Jesus is looking for good men and women today. "He [Jesus] chose the unlearned fishermen to be his disciples in order that they might learn of him, and become wise unto salvation. Why was it he did not choose the scribes and the Pharisees? It was because he could not trust them" (*Review and Herald*, Sept. 3, 1895). Can He trust us to finish what those first disciples started? He can if we will follow His leading.

"If men in humble life were encouraged to do all the good they could do, if restraining hands were not laid upon them to repress their zeal, there would be a hundred workers for Christ where now there is one. *God takes men as they are, and educates them for His service, if they will yield themselves to Him*" (*The Desire of Ages*, p. 251; italics supplied). In *Steps to Christ* she adds to the ratio: "If the followers of Christ were awake to duty, there would be thousands where there is one today proclaiming the gospel" (p. 81).

Today the Seventh-day Adventist Church is more than 10 million strong and growing 2,000 members a day. How long would it take us to finish the Great Commission of Matthew 28:18-20 if we *all* went to work? But that is not the point I want to make here. We can't worry about what the rest of the members are doing for Christ right now. All we can focus on—in fact, do anything about—is ourselves.

"If by our example we aid others in the development of good principles, we give them power to do good. In their turn they exert the same influence upon others, and they upon still others. Thus by our unconscious influence thousands may be blessed" (*Christ's Object Lessons,* p. 340).

I know you probably have heard this a thousand times before, but it is true. If we each would set a goal of winning just one person for Christ this year, we would double our membership by this time next year. How would you like to have your church double the size it is today? It can happen, but only if we each do our part.

Bill won others to Christ and influenced them to join the church, and he isn't even a member.

Not long ago Sandie and her son started attending the local Seventh-day Adventist church because of what she had heard about Adventists through her husband, Bill, a former member. Although no longer active in the church, he still believed in the Adventist message. After he witnessed to Sandie and explained what we believe and why, she witnessed to her son, Kurt, and soon both started attending the congregation in Tupelo, Mississippi. They started enjoying the Christian fellowship of the members there as well as what they learned about Jesus. It wasn't long until Kurt started witnessing to his wife, Tawana. Then they witnessed to their grandmother, Mary Ruth.

Today Kurt is studying to become a minister in the Seventh-day Adventist Church. He and Tawana have helped place a once-dying church back on track with its mission to spread the gospel into "all the world." They, along with many other members, take videos to homes for people to watch and pass out printed material, and Kurt planned an evangelistic series. It is impossible to tell how many will come to Christ because of the witnessing of a former member (who, by the way, is starting to attend church again). And he and his wife were baptized in March of 1999.

"There are many who need the ministration of loving Christian hearts. Many have gone down to ruin who might have been saved if their neighbors, common men and women, had put forth personal effort for them. Many are waiting to be personally addressed. *In the very family, the neighborhood, the town, where we live, there is work for us to do as missionaries for Christ.* If we are Christians, this work will be our delight. No sooner is one converted than there is born within him a desire to make known to others what a precious friend he has found in Jesus. The saving and sanctifying truth cannot be shut up in his heart" (*The Desire of Ages,* p. 141; italics supplied).

Chapter 11

How to Witness to a Sanguine

Paul WRITES an interesting passage in Romans: "I do not understand my own actions. For I do not do what I want, but I do the very thing I hate. . . . So then it is no longer I that do it, but sin which dwells within me. For I know that nothing good dwells within me, that is, in my flesh. I can will what is right, but I cannot do it. . . . Wretched man that I am! Who will deliver me from this body of death?" (Rom. 7:15-24, RSV).

In the next four chapters we'll examine how to witness to different temperaments. If we can better understand how and why people think and act the way they do, then we will be able to witness to them in a more opportune manner.

"The nearer we come to Jesus, and the more clearly we discern the purity of His character, the more clearly shall we see the exceeding sinfulness of sin, and the less shall we feel like exalting ourselves. There will be a continual reaching out of the soul after God, a continual, earnest, heart-breaking confession of sin and humbling of the heart before Him. At every advance step in our Christian experience our repentance will deepen. We shall know that our sufficiency is in Christ alone and shall make the apostle's confession our own: 'I know that in me (that is, in my flesh,) dwelleth no good thing.' 'God forbid that I should glory, save in the cross of our Lord Jesus Christ, by whom the world is crucified unto me, and I unto the world'" (*The Acts of the Apostles,* p. 561).

It is clear from Scripture and the writings of Ellen White that no good ever comes from us as humans. We are sinful through and through. Our actions are sinful, and even our prayers are selfish. The prophet Isaiah declared: "But we are all as an unclean thing, and all our righteousnesses are as filthy rags" (Isa. 64:6). If I understand that verse correctly, this even includes our natural talents and abilities.

A vital point that we need to make here is that our talents and abilities are part of our genetic makeup. Every person who has ever been born received a set of natural talents that will be with them their entire lifetime. The DNA both the mother and father contributed will determine it. "It will be well to remember that tendencies of character are transmitted from parents to children. . . . In the fear of God gird on the armor for a life conflict with hereditary tendencies" (*Testimonies for the Church,* vol. 4, p. 439).

Let me give an example of what I mean. My mother was born with musical ability. She can keep perfect time while playing the piano and singing. I, on the other hand, wasn't born with her vocal or piano-playing talent, but I do have the gift of rhythm. Ever since I can remember I grew up beating on things (but not people). I used to gather trash cans, coffee cans, fence rails, drinking glasses from the kitchen—you name it—and pound rhythm on them. I almost drove my parents crazy. By the time my father purchased my first set of drums, I had the ability to make beautiful music. (Only another drummer would understand that statement.) I loved to perform for myself and others. The sanguine temperament in me drove me to show off my natural talent and ability.

Before I go any further, let me mention again that I am fully aware of how many Christians feel about drums. I had one well-meaning saint tell me that I was going to be lost for enjoying drums. (They used another choice phrase for being lost that I do not care to repeat here.) Some sincere Christians believe that anyone who likes to play or hear music that has a drumbeat in it is doomed. (Does that mean King David will be lost then? Again and again you find him writing about percussion instruments and playing them. See 2 Samuel 6:5; 1 Chronicles 13:8; 15:16; and Psalm 150:3-5.)

I'm convicted that we can use any musical instrument for the glory of God or the delight of Satan, whether it be drums, pianos, organs, or guitars. However, let me add that I also believe each instrument has its time and place to be played. Personally I'm not comfortable having drums or electric guitars in the pulpit area, probably because I was raised with them not being there, but I would not condemn a church for having them. I believe one of the reasons celebration churches are so popular today is their livelier music. Let me stress that I personally believe the music played in God's house should do nothing less than uplift our heavenly Father and His Son, Jesus. And I hope by understanding our temperaments better, you will have a clearer understanding of why some enjoy one type of music more than another.

I am a natural-born drummer. It came easy for me. It illustrates the principle that every person has some sort of natural skill. That is why we have such great ball players, writers, musicians, speakers, etc. Sure, they have to practice, weed out weak points, build muscles, get their timing down, etc., but their skill came instinctively. None of it was by accident. It resulted from genetic traits passed on from generation to generation. I do not play the drums anymore (although I still like to beat on trash cans once in a while), but I have been able to take some of the skills I learned while performing on stage and use them for God today. Because of my natural performing aptitude that God gave me, I'm able to stand up in front of a congregation and not feel afraid. In fact, the more people present, the less nervous I am. In Russia I spoke to a crowd of more than 1,000 people who could not understand one word I said (and with my Texas accent, that may have been for the best). I preached as if I were standing in front of a mirror. But when it comes to one-on-one witnessing or preaching to a small congregation, it's a totally different story. I become nervous. While I still do it, I feel tense and apprehensive.

The same holds true with my ventriloquism. I enjoy teaching young people to "say no to drugs" using illusions and puppets. During the past five years I have spoken to more than 7,000 children in seven states, and I've spoken twice in Russia. I fell quite comfortable being in front of others with the dummy. In fact, the only time you will ever hear me sing (not one of my natural talents) is when I have one of my puppet friends beside me. (They do the singing, not me.) It doesn't bother me at all to have people laugh at *their* singing, but I could never sing by myself! That would be most embarrassing—not only to me, but also to everyone within listening range.

Because of my sanguine temperament, witnessing comes easily for me. I just be myself, and people sense that I genuinely care about them and their situation. I can start a conversation with just about anyone and talk about most subjects.

By now I'm sure you have been able to tell that a lot of my resources for this book come from personal experiences. Although I have researched and surveyed all the temperaments, I make no claims on being the final authority, because I still hold a firm belief that the best school for witnessing is on-the-job training! Ellen White says that "a general movement is needed, and this must begin *with individual movements*. In every church *let every member* of every family make determined efforts to deny self and to help forward the work. Let the children act a part. Let all cooperate. Let us do our best at this time to render to God our offering, to carry out His specified will, *and thus make an occasion for witnessing for Him and His truth in a world of darkness*. The lamp is in our hands. Let its light shine forth brightly" (*ibid.,* vol. 6, p. 470; italics supplied).

Being a sanguine and writing about how to witness to a sanguine will probably make this chapter the easiest for me to illustrate. Let's begin by looking at what makes a sanguine tick and see if we can understand why they do what they do best: have fun and make mistakes.

Sanguines have many strong capabilities. The life of the party, they never meet a stranger. They like to analyze things by opening up new data and using both open-ended and consensual approaches to examine information. Frequently they compromise by being willing to give in, in order to get what they want in the first place: approval. Leading by being tactful and flexible, they like to hear from other people how they personally are doing. People of a sanguine temperament need to know if everyone accepts what they are doing or saying. Although the first to volunteer for almost anything, they find it difficult to stick with the project.

Unfriendly people turn off sanguines, and they hate to be criticized. They despise routine, details, and strict schedules. Although they dislike being pressured into doing something, they'll do it anyway because they hope it will help them receive approval. It stresses them when they make promises they know they cannot deliver because they perceive that it will create disappointment and anger.

Here is a list of their strengths and weaknesses.*

Sanguine Strengths

1. Talkative and friendly
2. Compassionate
3. Physical touchers
4. Great storytellers and highly optimistic
5. Sincere and love everyone
6. Make friends easily
7. Can easily forgive others who have wronged them
8. Thrive on compliments
9. Great starters
10. Highly enthusiastic and can inspire anyone
11. Charismatic
12. Often called the idea people

Sanguine Weaknesses

1. Loud, compulsive talkers
2. Exaggerate and often seem phony
3. Emotionally unstable and naive
4. Want popularity
5. Constantly need an audience
6. Make excuses whenever something goes wrong
7. Weak-willed
8. Unorganized
9. Easily distracted
10. Undisciplined
11. Forgetful and fickle

Some characteristic traits of sanguines are:

Strengths

1. Use a light touch and personal charm to win people over
2. Sensitive to others' feelings and what will please them
3. Flexible in finding ways to satisfy other people
4. Fit in easily with different people
5. Quick to change and adapt to new ideas and ways

Weaknesses

1. Can be overly entertaining and distracting in serious situations
2. May lose sight of their own course and not do what's best, thus feeling unappreciated later
3. Accommodate wishes of others too much and may switch sides on issues
4. May get overinvolved in socializing and not utilize their time efficiently
5. Can lose sight of goals

Sanguines are often easy and enjoyable to work with.

They can and will do a good job if they know they are appreciated and liked. Here is a short list of ways to influence and motivate sanguines into giving you their all.

1. Give them opportunities to work with others.

2. Use humorous appeals that make them laugh.

3. Let them know when you are pleased with their work and be tactful when you are not.

4. Provide as many opportunities for them to be in the spotlight as possible.

Here is a list of how you can be the most effective leader to sanguines and help them work to their full potential.

1. Always be friendly and informal.

2. Give helpful feedback and always begin with the positive aspects of their performance.

3. Clarify their role in the overall plan of things.

4. Try showing them as much flexibility as possible.

5. Try to display a sense of humor with them. They love it!

Sanguines are great at volunteering, and love to have others volunteer with them as long as it doesn't take them out of the spotlight. Here is a small list of ways you can be the most effective volunteer for a sanguine.

1. Always be sociable and tactful.

2. Learn to keep things light and humorous, because they hate serious situations.

3. Try to demonstrate how you can fit in with their purpose and make them look better.

Their most effective working environment has the following characteristics:

1. Social

2. Flexible

3. Informal

4. Accepting

Least effective environment:

1. Unfriendly coworkers

2. Critical or overbearing coworkers

3. Authoritative people and surroundings

4. Routines and details

5. Firm schedules and supervision

"More than one thousand will soon be converted in one day, most of whom will trace their first convictions to the reading of our publications" (*Evangelism,* p. 693). Sanguines are highly emotional when they read. Many come to God because of their convictions, but they must be worked with daily to maintain them.

Strengths sanguines will bring to the church:

1. Keep in touch with people's strengths and feelings

2. Use a light touch and take the strain out of serious situations

3. Good at demonstrating flexibility and making workable compromises

4. Great at getting others excited about new ideas and keeping up interest in old ones

5. Good at adopting goals and facilitating efforts

6. Make perfect greeters

Sanguines' views of others

Other sanguines:

1. Faked out too often

2. Feel as if they have been fooled

3. Promises can't be trusted

4. Don't take problems seriously

Cholerics:

1. Locked into their viewpoint
2. Aren't tuned in to others
3. Too demanding and uncaring
4. Don't heed other people's reactions

Melancholies:

1. Too serious
2. Too pious
3. Too critical
4. Too problem-oriented

Phlegmatics:

1. Too controlled to be real
2. No regard for people's feelings
3. Too rigid (stubborn)
4. Too possessive

Florence Littauer has some good counsel on knowing how to understand a sanguine better that, if heeded, will make it easier to witness to many of them. "The sanguine who appears on the surface to be happy in any situation is, underneath, longing for attention, acceptance, and approval. Sanguines need to know they are loved and that you accept them just as they are. They want an audience who applauds and they wilt under criticism and poor reviews" (*Your Personality Tree*, p. 63).

In chapter 6 we talked about old habits coming back easier for some people than others. Sanguines have the hardest struggle in this area. Their combination of an outgoing personality and a constant need for attention makes them have a difficult time keeping their eyes focused on always doing what is right. You might classify them as the *rule breakers* of the church. Sad as it is to say, not many churches today make room for *rule breakers*. Because they ignore rules and regulations, they slip easily into Satan's traps again and again. They are the first to be inspired at an evangelistic series and feel the need to be baptized—and the first of the temperaments to leave the church. Or they may be the first to stop smoking and the first to start back up before the night is over.

It takes time and a lot of patience to work with sanguines. We need to study with them in such a way that we bring the Scriptures alive for them. They love hearing and telling Bible stories, but you should stay away from heavy doctrines and prophecy at first. Center on God's forgiveness and love for them personally. Use Bible examples such as Peter being forgiven after denying he knew Christ. Sanguines need to know that God loves them unconditionally and that Jesus will forgive them completely. Give them time to talk, even if they keep getting off the topic you're studying. And remember, you may have to repeat the same topic again and again before it finally sinks in. Sanguines are good at hearing what you say today but will forget it completely by next week. Hang in there with sanguines, because if they give their hearts fully to Christ, they will make fine workers for God.

"The sincerity of Mr. Sanguine is often misunderstood by others. They are deceived by his sudden changes of emotion, and they fail to understand that he is genuinely responding to the emotions of others. No one can love you more nor forget you faster than sanguines. The world is enriched by these cheerful, responsive people. When motivated and disciplined by God, they can be great servants of Jesus Christ" (*Why You Act the Way You Do,* p. 62).

Now that you know the needs of a sanguine, hopefully

you will have a better understanding of how to reach them for God.

---

*Much of the material about temperaments has been adapted from Len McMillan, Ph.D., family life director at the Pacific Health Education Center in Bakersfield, California. Used by permission.

Chapter 12

How to Witness to a Melancholy

By NOW I hope you have come to the conclusion that by learning the underlying needs of each temperament you can and will better understand human relationships. Because I wanted this book to be as accurate as possible, I asked different people, Christian and non-Christian, male and female, of different temperaments to explain to me how others had witnessed to them. I wanted to know what worked personally for them and what did not. Also, I asked what would make them feel comfortable, where they would want others to approach them, and what they would want said if they could be witnessed to all over again. Throughout this book I have shared many of their thoughts with you.

It is next to impossible for me to write or preach on topics I know nothing or very little about, even if they are of great importance. Yet unfortunately, as I study different authors and listen to different speakers, I see them doing it all the time. And I believe this is wrong. Not only is it difficult for me to explain how to do something I myself have never done; it is also laborious for those listening to accept it. Many think, *How would you know how easy or difficult it is, since you have never walked in my shoes before?*

For example: I get extremely upset whenever I hear someone lecture on how easy it is to quit smoking, using drugs, or drinking when they have never touched any of the substances. All they know is what they have read in some instruction manual and/or heard from others who did quit.

I've attended several stop-smoking seminars during which the facilitator admitted (proudly, I might add) that he had never smoked a cigarette in his life. Sometimes they have the nerve to stand up front and pronounce that anyone can quit smoking if they truly want to, and that it will be easy and fun. And if that isn't enough, such people declare that once an individual has stopped, the craving will never return. Being a former smoker, I know how difficult it was for me to stop and stay stopped. I quit smoking three times before I was able to break the habit completely. (Remember, I'm a sanguine.) Yes, the craving did leave after a while, but for years the devil tempted me with the desire to resume smoking. Many nights I would have nightmares about my smoking again that were so real that I woke up in a cold sweat. Satan would whisper in my ears that smoking was "cool" and made me look macho, a "real *he*-man." It has been only by the grace of God and keeping a strong relationship with Jesus each day that I have been able to stay off cigarettes, liquor, and drugs the past two decades. And it will be only by the same grace that I remain off. It wasn't easy for me and it sure wasn't fun, but I do praise God for victory.

Another example would be for me or any man, for that matter, to preach, write, or teach exactly how a woman feels about any subject. I have never walked in a woman's shoes and never will. It is impossible for me to understand a woman's *true* feelings completely and fully. All I know is what I've read and heard from women explaining to me how they respond to different topics. And let's face facts—it is difficult for any male preacher or counselor to understand and help a woman who has come to him for advice. We men can understand things only from a male point of view. Whenever I counsel a woman, I have to draw on what I've learned from my studies and previous counseling sessions with other women. That is why I often ask my female counselees if they would mind if my wife sat in on some of our sessions. She can understand from a woman's point of view and try to help me grasp the counselee's frustration and hurt.

And the same principle holds true in trying to write about different temperaments. It was easy for me to do the previous chapter, "How to Witness to a Sanguine." The same was true of the chapter "How to Witness to a Phlegmatic," since that is my secondary temperament. But this chapter and the next one are a totally different story. It is baffling and difficult for me to explain *exactly* how to witness to cholerics and melancholies when I do not have any idea how they *actually* feel inside. Sure, I know what the books and psychologists say, but I have never walked in a choleric's or melancholy's shoes. That is why much of what you find in this book about cholerics and melancholies comes from my personal surveys, investigation, and studies; from witnessing to many of them in the past; and from the experience of being married to a melancholy.

Recently I asked a number of men if they would rather have been born a woman. Without exception (and I say this kindly), every man I interviewed was thankful he had not. All but one woman responded in the negative when I asked whether they would have rather have been born a man. And the one woman that did say she wished she had been born a man is a phlegmatic and has a problem making decisions.

The same held true when I asked about being born with a different temperament. Again everyone, male and female, said they were glad they were born with the personality and temperament they have—weaknesses and all. (Although two melancholy women commented that they wished they had a little more sanguine in them.) My survey demonstrated to me that it is easier for us to accept and understand ourselves than to accept and understand others. Because we can't understand why others do what they do, say what they say, and act the way they act, many of us become more content with ourselves every day, imperfections and all.

When you glance at the letters section in most magazines you will notice how many people disagree with each other. As I read the letters section in a recent *Adventist Review* I couldn't help recognizing that many of our members do not see eye-to-eye on every subject (as if you didn't already know that). One or more persons would agree wholeheartedly with the author of an article, and others would seem to be screaming at the writer through their printed letter or implying that the author must be an ignoramus.

Have you ever wondered why everyone doesn't agree with each other and see eye-to-eye on every subject? Why is it that we would not have wanted to be born the opposite gender or with another temperament? Why is it that we almost always feel that "I'm right and you're wrong" when it comes to a topic, even when we have little knowledge about it? How is it that two people can read the same passage of Scripture and arrive at totally different views of what God is saying? How can there be so many different denominations that use the same Bible, yet do not perceive and understand God's Word in the same way?

I believe the answer to these questions and many more is found in understanding the temperaments. Each one of us is as different as one snowflake is from another. That is another reason I regard knowing and understanding the temperaments as vital to witnessing. When we better grasp what a person is thinking, then we are at an advantage in leading the individual into knowing and understanding the truths of God's Word. We can use their own words, opinions, and thoughts to help explain the Bible in terms that will make sense to them.

Recently I went as the pastor of a mission trip to South Dakota. We presented a Vacation Bible School on a Native American reservation. While there I came to know many of the local Lakota Sioux church members. It was remarkable to listen during Sabbath school to the stories they grew up with. Many of the tales sounded like Bible stories, only with a different twist. One of the most touching and yet saddest stories I've ever heard concerned how the Christians came to them centuries ago intending to convert them. The Christians wanted the Native Americans to give up everything they believed in—their way of life and culture. They expected the Native Americans to be just like them—the way they dressed, the food they ate, and the homes they lived in. Everything! The missionaries instructed the Native Americans that they could keep none of their culture if they were to become Christians. Today if you were to visit a reservation, you would see the results of that mistake. Many Native Americans want nothing to do with the "White man's religion." Why? Because we tried to take away their way of life and thinking.

Now, I'm not saying that they did not have to give up their sins. The Bible is quite clear on what sin is. But we tried to turn them into Whites. It didn't work centuries ago and it still won't today. The same holds true in trying to make a sanguine study like a melancholy or a phlegmatic like a choleric. We will drive away, rather than save, those we are trying to witness to. Christ never sought to make the Gentiles into Jews.

Every time you read about Jesus speaking to someone about salvation, you will notice that Jesus met them on their level. He went to wedding parties (John 2), ate with sinners and publicans (Luke 19), and had private meetings at night (John 3). Our Saviour tried to help His disciples and the Pharisees to see others from a totally different view than they had been bought up with. And Jesus wanted *everyone* to be accepted into His fold just as they were and then given time to grow. With time, prayer, love, and patience, He would change them. "Therefore being justified by faith, we have peace with God through our Lord Jesus Christ" (Rom. 5:1). "Being justified freely by his grace through the redemption that is in Christ Jesus: whom God hath set forth to be a propitiation through faith in his blood, to declare his righteousness for the remission of sins that are past, through the forbearance of God" (Rom. 3:24, 25). "Blessed are they whose iniquities are forgiven, and whose sins are covered. Blessed is the man to whom the Lord will not impute sin" (Rom. 4:7, 8). "Until we all reach unity in the faith and in the knowledge of the Son of God and become mature, attaining to the whole measure of the fullness of Christ" (Eph. 4:13, NIV). We don't change people; God does. But until He has completely transformed them, we are to love and accept them for who and what they are.

The temperament that seems to have the greatest difficulty seeing eye-to-eye on any subject, that has the tendency not to want to give others time to grow, and that expects everyone to be just like them is the melancholy. They cannot grasp why others would do a job halfway, and don't mind telling them so. Melancholies are the ones who will search and find the much-needed mistake in a lawyer's case. They continue even though they appear to be looking for a needle in a haystack, because they recognize that many court cases can be turned around on just a single word. This particular temperament examines for details and enjoys scrutinizing every project before it even begins.

Probably melancholies are the hardest to determine what they are thinking because they have the bad habit of telling you that everything is all right when, in fact, it isn't. Florence Littauer bluntly states that "melancholies lie." If I ask a melancholy if something is wrong and he or she replies no, everything is all right, I know something is wrong.

Earlier I observed that melancholies have the richest of all the temperaments. They are the analytical, self-sacrificing, gifted perfectionists with a highly sensitive emotional nature. By their very nature melancholies are prone to be introverted, but since their true feelings predominate, they experience a variety of moods. These moods at times can lift them to heights of ecstasy and cause them to appear more extroverted than they really are.

One of my favorite pastimes is trying to guess what temperament a person might be the moment I meet them and then later see if I'm right. Sometimes after I really get to know a person I realize that I have guessed wrong. And it is almost always a melancholy that I had pegged as a sanguine. Both melancholies and sanguines make great actors, because they can put on a disguise and camouflage their true feelings.

It wasn't until I understood the temperaments better that I came to realize that the melancholy often wears a mask. They hide behind them because they do not want anyone to know the real person they presume they are. Instead, they assume that if they show their true face, no one will really like them. Melancholies do not want anyone to find out that they are hurting and depressed inside. But unlike a sanguine, a melancholy doesn't make friends easily. Not liking to make the first move, they wait for others to approach them. I have found some to be touchy, laugh a lot, tell jokes, and volunteer for almost everything, but inside they struggle with pain, discouragement, and depression.

Perhaps one of the greatest strengths of melancholies is that they are the most dependable of all the temperaments. Because of their perfectionistic tendencies, they will not disappoint others or let them down.

Where the sanguine might stretch the truth, the melancholy will hold to the exact facts. They are highly detailed with their facts and figures. Some have labeled them as the "detail hounds." This tendency can drive you insane when you attempt to get a simple yes or no answer. I remember years ago asking a friend of mine a simple question about the Bible, and it took him almost 10 minutes before he finally answered me. Wanting to make sure I knew and understood all the background on who did what and how, he laid out all the facts and figures starting in Genesis and ending in Revelation. But all I wanted was a yes or no reply. By the time he got around to answering my question, I had forgotten what I had asked.

Whereas the cholerics are the *"rule makers"* and sanguines are the *"rule breakers"* of the church, the melancholies are the *"rule keepers."* They're perfectly happy keeping the rules and laws and perhaps "have the most consistent, active and extensive prayer life. They pray about everything! They truly enjoy communion with God. Like the prophets, melancholies are most likely to schedule a specific time each day with God and truly look forward to that appointment" (*Ministry,* January 1997, p. 19).

"Spirit-filled melancholies are unstoppable, but self-conscious melancholies are unstartable. Naturally endowed with analytical skills, perfectionistic melancholies often become the depressed church members you are called upon to encourage. Not able to live up to their own expectations, melancholies find it difficult to believe that God can love them with their imperfections. Feeling unworthy, pessimistic melancholies often plead 'Why me?' The optimistic cry of the sanguines and cholerics tends to be 'Why not me?'" (*ibid.*).

Here is a short list of their strengths and weaknesses.

Melancholy Strengths
    1. Highly sensitive and creative

2. Conscientious and idealistic

3. Have deep concern for others

4. Analytical

5. Like to keep on schedule

6. Very orderly

7. Need to finish what they start

8. Faithful

9. Perfectionistic

10. Self-sacrificing

11. Good listeners

12. Oriented to goals and drives

Melancholy Weaknesses

1. Strong persecution complex that can cause guilt

2. Low self-esteem leading to insecurity

3. Cud chewers (see story later in this chapter)

4. False humility; often feel like martyrs

5. Highly task oriented

6. Set too high standards for themselves and others

7. Need approval

8. Skeptical of compliments

9. Suspicious of others

Some characteristic traits of melancholies are:

Strengths

1. Have to feel they are working on the best, most relevant project

2. Like to be achievers, doing something to benefit people

3. Willing to trust the statements of others at face value

4. Make allowances for people and defend their rights

5. Allow others to feel important in determining direction of what's happening

Weaknesses

1. Reluctant to work on less relevant projects

2. Can get overinvolved in other people's problems

3. Easily manipulated, leading to disappointment in people

4. Overprotective and oversympathetic with the interests of others

5. May be too responsive to the directions of others, and may find it difficult to initiate action

"It seems easier to challenge a melancholy to a lifetime of service for Jesus than any other temperament" (*Why You Act the Way You Do*, p. 103).

Here is a short list of ways to influence and motivate melancholies into cooperating:

1. Stress worthwhile causes

2. Appeal to principles

3. Ask for help

4. Appeal to excellence

5. Show concern

6. Stress self-development

Here is a list of ways you can be the most effective leader to melancholies:

1. Give them recognition

2. Allow mutual goal-setting

3. Always be accessible

4. Be dependable

5. Try to share

6. Acknowledge your trust in them

How to be the best volunteer for melancholies:

1. Demonstrate worth
2. Show loyalty
3. Be sincere
4. Be team-oriented

"Melancholies don't need a great deal of long-suffering and self-control, for if their motivation is oriented by the Spirit of God and they are instructed by the Word of God, they make extremely effective Christian workers known not for their flamboyant style, but for their self-sacrificing consistent spirit" (*ibid.*, p. 103).

The most effective type of environment for melancholies should be:

1. Respecting
2. Supportive
3. Reassuring
4. Idealistic

Least effective environment for melancholies:

1. Betrayal
2. Anything personal and hostile to them as individuals
3. Criticism
4. Ridicule
5. Failure
6. Lack of support

Strengths melancholies will bring to the church:

1. Keeping an eye on quality
2. Maintaining excellence
3. Keeping relevant goals in focus
4. Getting cooperation from others
5. Being responsive to the needs of others and supportive of a good cause

6. Comparing the past with the present and projecting it into the future

7. Being among the best musicians and theologians

To communicate with volunteers who are melancholy:

1. Focus on excellence

2. Appeal to principles

3. Set goals together

4. Stress worthy causes

To communicate with leaders who are melancholy:

1. Demonstrate worth

2. Show loyalty

3. Think of others

4. Be a team member

Melancholies' views of others

Sanguines:

1. Too flexible

2. Cannot be trusted

3. Without principles

4. Not serious or involved enough

Cholerics:

1. Too overbearing/ruthless

2. Unwilling to learn

3. Unprincipled

4. Overly demanding

5. Make one feel inadequate

Other Melancholies:

1. Make one feel guilty

2. Misunderstand

3. Tend to disappoint

4. Don't trust them

Phlegmatics:

1. Too cautious
2. Too tied to ritual and procedure
3. Don't express feelings or care for people
4. Too withdrawn

Len McMillan compares melancholies to the cud-chewing cow. A cow will chew its food and swallow it, placing it in one compartment of its stomach, only to later regurgitate it and chew on it again. Then it will swallow the food and place it in another compartment of the stomach before bringing it back up and chewing on it some more. The animal will continue the procedure until the food is completely digested.

The melancholy does the same thing with situations that hurt or disappoint them. They will chew on the issue for a while, then swallow it, only to later bring it back up and chew on it some more. They can tell you the time of day it happened, the location, and the clothes that everyone wore. And the melancholy will continue rehashing the problem for a long time.

By nature melancholies are self-centered and tend toward perfectionism, making them impatient with the habits and carelessness of others. When working with a melancholy, remember that joy is an absolute necessity. Happiness helps them replace their natural bent toward remorse and mood swings.

When melancholies encounter stress they will assume responsibility and try harder, but often become critical of self and others when they cannot achieve the impossible.

Here are some tips on how melancholies handle conflict:

1. Are willing to hear the positions of others

2. May overidentify with someone else's objectives instead of their own

3. Will accept and try to solve legitimate complaints

4. May accept unreasonable demands

5. Willing to extend self to do what is right and fair by others

6. Become self-denying and make too many concessions

7. High commitment to reducing conflict and establishing cooperation

8. Will give in to opposition rather than be seen as uncooperative

9. Will influence opposition through statements of principle and fairness

10. Moralistic, often reciting the injustice done to them

"It has long been a mystery to me that those melancholy individuals who are endowed by their Creator with the greatest number of talents seem to have the least confidence in themselves. This is probably due to their everlasting tendency toward self-criticism and self-condemnation" (*ibid.,* pp. 102, 103).

I have noticed that when the Holy Spirit enters the heart of melancholies, He literally transforms them. "The peace of the Holy Spirit is a welcome tonic to the melancholy, whose inner thoughts fluctuate from criticism and condemnation, to hostility and revenge, and back to suspicion and fear" (*ibid.,* p. 104).

Go slowly and show facts when studying with a melancholy. They want to see a "Thus saith the Lord" explanation. Picky eaters, they take forever to make up their mind when ordering from a menu. The same holds true when studying the Bible. Very picky when it comes to God's Word, they will not accept a "Well, I think it's in the Bible somewhere" answer. Instead, they want to read it and see it for themselves. Examining the text, they break it down, study, and chew on it for a while. And once convinced and convicted, they will guard that truth with their life.

As a general rule, no other temperament has a higher IQ or is more creative and has a greater imagination. No one else is as capable of such high-quality work as a melancholy.

God probably used more melancholies in the writing of the Bible than any other temperament, because no other has as much natural potential when energized by the Holy Spirit.

It would do well for the melancholy to remember that "the Christian life is a battle and a march. Let us go forward, for we are striving for an immortal crown. Let us give diligence to make our calling and election sure. We shall triumph at last, if we do not become weary in well-doing" (*Review and Herald,* Nov. 29, 1887).

Chapter 13

How to Witness to a Choleric

Not all can be helped in the same way. God deals with each according to his temperament and character, and we must cooperate with Him" (*Gospel Workers,* p. 208). "We must bear with one another, remembering our failings. With some have compassion, making a difference; others save with fear, pulling them out of the fire. All cannot bear the same rigid discipline. All cannot be brought up to just another's ideas of duty. Allowance must be made for different temperaments and different minds" (*Mind, Character, and Personality,* vol. 2, pp. 632, 633).

Isn't it amazing how we can so badly misread someone unless we fully understand their basic personalities and their underlying needs? That is why unless we have some understanding of the temperaments we will find that the choleric type person can be the hardest to accept and understand.

I have discovered that witnessing to cholerics can be fun and exciting if I understand their way of thinking. Whenever I approach a choleric to study God's Word, I soon discover that many are ecstatic and thrilled to jump right into a study with me. But many will do so with guns and ammunition strapped to their sides. They may never plan to use them, however, unless for some reason or another I disagree with them.

It seems that cholerics have a strong inclination to want to study end-time prophecy and the signs of Jesus' second coming. They like to know what is going to happen to them and the world as we know it. When it comes to knowing and keeping the commandments of God's Word, they can resemble the Pharisees. That is why they are sometimes known as the *"rule makers"* of the church, believing and preaching that God gave us the Ten Commandments as only a starting point of His laws and ways. They feel it their sacred duty to formulate new policies and rules for themselves and others to follow. Cholerics like it when everyone walks a tightrope, keeps a tidy ship, and allows them to be the ship's captain. Listen to how Ellen White addresses a person that fits this description:

"Sometimes a man who has been placed in responsibility as a leader gains the idea that he is in a position of supreme authority, and that all his brethren, before making advance moves, must first come to him for permission to do that which they feel should be done. Such a man is in a dangerous position. He has lost sight of the work of a true leader among God's people. Instead of acting as a wise counselor, he assumes the prerogatives of an exacting ruler. God is dishonored by every such display of authority and self-exaltation. No man standing in his own strength is ever to be mind and judgment for another man whom the Lord is using in His work. *No one is to lay down man-made rules and regulations to govern arbitrarily his fel-*

low laborers who have a living experience in the truth" (*Testimonies to Ministers,* p. 491; italics supplied). Here is what I view as the choleric's greatest weakness.

A few chapters earlier we discussed many good and much-needed strengths of the choleric, and we will examine even more in this chapter. But first I would like to review some of their weaknesses again. Weaknesses that if not given over to the Holy Spirit can and will destroy many lives, including their own.

Cholerics are the inherent pacesetters, often good judges of people, and quick to respond to an emergency. Able to take charge of virtually any situation, they direct others to react quickly. They will do whatever it takes to get the task done their way. If they realize kindness will accomplish what they want, then they'll try that. But many cholerics know that standing their ground and pounding the table a little harder with their fist works the best in achieving what they want unless they face another strong choleric. Then watch the sparks fly.

Whenever any one type of personality dominates a congregation, you'll soon discover some of the other members defending their convictions. And all too often it is the choleric governing the church and its members that causes the battle. I have been in churches in which I sensed a power struggle the moment I walked in the door, and I could feel unkind Christian behavior.

Years ago an elder had such a strong choleric nature that he seemed to run the whole congregation. He knew that if he screamed loud and long enough, he would get his way. And he did. Not until his death did the church ever start growing again. Another congregation I am familiar with for years had such a strong choleric elder as its leader that the church finally died, closed its doors, and sold the church building. In both cases the leaders governed God's church the way they wanted it ruled, and because they would not listen to advice or counsel, God's people suffered. And I'm sure that you are familiar with many more cases.

I used to wonder if something ought to be said to those who want to control God's church. I wanted to inform them that I didn't believe they were acting as Christ would. But knowing how a person with a choleric temperament might respond, I held back (a weakness of my own temperament). While preparing this chapter, I ran across the following counsel: "Sometimes a case presents itself that should be made a prayerful study. *The person must be shown his true character, understand his own peculiarities of disposition and temperament, and see his infirmities.* He should be judiciously handled" (*Testimonies for the Church,* vol. 4, p. 69; italics supplied).

Sometimes when certain members try to dominate God's church, we must confront them and explain that we truly care, understand, and believe that they have only what is best for God's church in mind, but that they must also allow others to voice their opinions. Always we must approach them in love, and then never until we have sought advice from God in prayer. Although some may not listen to our advice at first, a true born-again choleric will seek God's counsel and allow Him to lead.

We will find that when cholerics fully yield their will to the Holy Spirit, their easily triggered feelings, thoughts, and hostile actions will be replaced with love, understanding, kindness, and gentleness. But we must also keep in mind that sometimes it takes a while for such changes to become permanent.

Restricted resources and having no challenges seem to turn cholerics off. Detesting people that attempt to under-cut them, they like to plan as they go along, and they love to strike hard bargains with just about anyone. They quickly respond to urgent appeals and opportunities, but many times they will use their authority or position when leading others to force them to "do what I say; I know what's best."

When it comes to communicating with others, a choleric wants to know what are the opportunities, what is the bottom line, who's in control, and what happens next. Cholerics are difficult to please, but as long as they are kept busy working, they seem to be happy.

Here is a short list of their strengths and weaknesses.

Choleric Strengths
1. Strong-willed and aggressive
2. Dynamic and born to lead
3. Independent and practical
4. Goal-oriented
5. Excel during emergencies
6. Usually right in their decision-making
7. Good at choosing and delegating
8. Great organizers

Choleric Weaknesses
1. Bossy and often earn reputations as cruel taskmasters
2. Quick-tempered and can explode in a split second
3. Argumentative and proud
4. Arrogant and domineering

5. Manipulate people

6. Find apologizing difficult

7. Workaholics

8. Can be rude and tactless

9. Bored by trivia

Some characteristic traits of cholerics are:

Strengths

1. Like to be in control and steer the course of events

2. Quick to act and express a sense of urgency for others to act now

3. Enjoy the challenge of difficult situations and people

4. Like a quick pace and a fast track; enjoy variety, novelty, and new projects

5. Probe and press to get at hidden resistance

6. Quick to move in and seize opportunity or to create one

Weaknesses

1. Dominate and cut off expression of important data by others

2. Sacrifice thought for action and may overwhelm others with feelings of emergency

3. May take challenge for challenge's sake when to do so is not productive

4. May not pay enough attention to maintain continued success of old projects

5. Can make others feel victims of "third degree"

6. May try to force action when none is needed

Cholerics have been known to be extremely difficult to work with. They insist on action and often offer unsolicited advice, such as "Here's what I'd do if I were in your shoes!" They like to take charge and initiate all ground rules and will use their authority to their advantage to get what they want done. But they can and will perform well if they know they are in control.

Here is a short list of ways to influence and motivate cholerics into cooperating:

1. Give them more responsibility.
2. Offer them challenges.
3. Provide them with the resources they need to achieve.
4. Let them delegate authority when possible.
5. Offer them opportunities.

Here is a list of how you can be the most effective leader to cholerics.

1. Always be confident of them.
2. Provide them autonomy and independence.
3. Reward results.
4. Set firm boundaries.
5. Appreciate their initiative.
6. Discuss matters with them on an equal basis.

Cholerics are great at volunteering and will allow others to work alongside them as long as they are in charge. Here is a brief list of how you can be the most effective volunteer for cholerics:

1. Be responsive.
2. Demonstrate competence.
3. Show independence.
4. Be direct.

Their most effective environment:

1. Anyplace involving competition, because they are highly competitive

2. A place that involves risk-taking

Their least effective environment:

1. Areas that have restricted resources

2. Situations in which others have more authority than they do

3. Situations in which they have diminished responsibility

4. Situations in which they have no challenges

5. Situations in which they have no control over results

Strengths that cholerics will bring to the church:

1. Create a sense of urgency to get things started

2. Sense opportunities

3. Willing to confront and bargain hard for a fair share

4. Able to organize others and take charge of uncertain situations

5. Able to stay with a difficult situation to prove that it can be done

To communicate with choleric volunteers:

1. Focus on action

2. Provide autonomy

3. Stress opportunity

4. Offer them challenges

To communicate with choleric leaders:

1. Initiate

2. Be responsive

3. Show competence

4. Talk the "bottom line"

Cholerics' views of others

Sanguines:

1. Too tricky

2. Too solicitous (anxious, concerned, eager)

3. Not dependable

Other cholerics:

1. Too feisty
2. Too impulsive
3. Go beyond limits too often
4. Cannot be controlled
5. Leave no room for others

Melancholies:

1. Too needy
2. Not action-oriented enough
3. Too soft
4. Their heads seem to be in the clouds

Phlegmatics:

1. Too slow to react
2. Bogged down in details
3. Overly cautious
4. They curb what cholerics want to do, which slows them down

When cholerics become stressed, they will often throw intense energy in several directions simultaneously and overextend themselves. They will respond without checking policies or clearing anything with those in authority.

Should a conflict arise, they will state their position firmly and with strong conviction. And unless they permit the Holy Spirit to lead, they can sound arrogant and demanding, which will only frustrate others. Often they overemphasize their disagreement, making it difficult for others to cope with them.

Cholerics are hard-driving workers who don't know what the word "quit" means. They seem to others not to have an ounce of emotional feeling or any needs and can be extremely insensitive to the needs of other people. By nature they can be very self-disciplined, long-suffering, strong-willed, determined, goal-oriented, and persistent. And because of this part of their temperament, the born-again choleric is most likely to follow Jesus with great energy and consistency.

No 'one can be more harsh and cantankerous than a choleric. Full of self-confidence, they desperately need the filling of the Holy Spirit, like the sanguines, to help to control their tongues. They need to learn to love others unconditionally and show compassion. Because of their naturally insensitive spirit, they can be a real challenge for the Holy Spirit to reach, and they need the peace that only God can give. But when they find that peace, they can be a most helpful tool for the Holy Spirit to use.

I believe Tim LaHaye says best how to understand the thinking of a choleric: "Rocky Choleric is a natural motivator of other people. He oozes self-confidence, is extremely goal-conscious, and can inspire others to envision his goals. Consequently, associates may find themselves more productive by following the choleric's lead. His primary weakness as a leader is that he is hard to please and tends to run roughshod over other people. If he only knew how others look to him for approval and encouragement, he would spend more time patting them on the back, which would generate even greater dedication from them. But the choleric subconsciously thinks that approval and encouragement will lead to complacency; he assumes that an employee's productivity will fall off if he is too complimentary. So he resorts to criticism in the hope that this will inspire greater effort. Unfortunately it doesn't" (*Spirit-controlled Temperament*, p. 23).

At times it may be good that cholerics can be hard-headed and like to debate, because when convinced of something from God's Word, they will defend it to death. Once they make a firm commitment to the Lord, you can bank on their standing true to that belief. When they join God's church they make a firm decision to stay and quickly advance up the ladder of leadership, holding key offices. They have a built-in ability to make good ministers, elders, deacons, and deaconesses. Once Spirit-controlled, they will lead God's church to new dimensions. Dynamic Bible teachers, they possess organization and promotional abilities and are not afraid to launch into new projects. With the proper motivation and the Lord's blessing, such projects will be highly successful.

Cholerics are among the first to stop smoking and drinking and will remain free of such habits indefinitely. But they cannot understand why everyone else can't quit cold turkey as they themselves did.

They can be easy to study with unless you hit a subject that they believe they have all the right answers to. At this point, just listen to them and give them time to explain their understanding of what God's Word says. Prayerfully and slowly ask them to consider different verses on the same topic. Try to get them to think about what the author of the passage is seeking to say. Gently lead them into different thoughts and beliefs on the subject at hand. Then allow them to voice their opinion again.

Although cholerics may have many weaknesses, the bottom line is that they just want their life and everyone else's under control. They feel they have the right answers to life's most difficult questions. When led by God's Holy

Spirit, they make great forerunners who can prepare the way for others to follow. We need our cholerics with their God-given talents. In fact, many of the great leaders of the Bible were choleric.

I pray that as you study with cholerics you will allow the Holy Spirit to lead and anoint your own lips to say the right words at the right time. As with all temperaments, if you cannot explain God's Word in a way that they understand, then find someone of the same temperament as theirs to study with them. Remember, we must work and witness within the other person's temperament—the temperament that God gave them.

"Give love to them that need it most. The most unfortunate, those who have the most disagreeable temperaments need our love, our tenderness, our compassion. Those who try our patience need most love" (*Fundamentals of Christian Education,* p. 281).

Chapter 14

How to Witness to a Phlegmatic

THERE ARE those who want more definite light than they receive from hearing the sermons. *Some need a longer time than do others to understand the points presented.* If the truth presented could be made a little plainer, they would see it and take hold of it, and it would be like a nail fastened in a sure place" (*Testimonies for the Church,* vol. 6, p. 87; italics supplied).

Through years of reading and studying various types of books and articles, I've noticed that a person can tell a little about the author's temperament and personality through the writing style. When we stop and examine the words, opinions, views, and thoughts, we often find that most authors write on themes that have a special meaning to them. But what guarantee do we have that the topic will have significance to us? How do we know that we will arrive at the same conclusion as the writer did?

Have you ever attended a book sale or camp meeting auction and purchased a book that someone promoted in a way that made it sound just like the very one you needed? It was advertised to cure your problems and give you a whole new outlook on life. But when you started reading it, you were not able to finish the first chapter before your mind started to drift off. That has happened to me all too often. I have shelves full of books in my office that I have purchased and never finished reading because the promoters (usually ABC managers) declared that it was the book for me. They'll proclaim that it's the perfect book for pastors and laypersons alike and that everyone should read it. Some promoters make me feel guilty if I don't secure one. But the problem I have with some books is that I can't always understand everything the author is trying to communicate. As a result I become bored and soon find myself placing it on the shelf with the other books. Why? Because not *all* books are written for *all* people. Each author speaks, preaches, teaches, witnesses, and writes in his or her particular, unique, and different style. That is why some may not understand what the author is trying to convey. Authors may wish and even pray that everyone could read, accept, and understand their book, but that is rarely the case.

I myself do not preach or witness like a choleric or melancholy. I know this because when someone comments on one of my sermons about something they didn't understand or like, it is usually an individual of one of those temperaments. Not everyone will read this book. And some who do purchase it will not get past chapter 1. Why? Because they may not feel impressed or believe that understanding how someone thinks will help them witness to others. Or because my writing style didn't appeal to them. It's like the old phrase says: "Different strokes for different folks."

This may also be why some would rather give away *The Great Controversy* than *The Desire of Ages*. One book appeals more to their heart than the other, although they may feel that both are excellent. Yet both volumes have won millions of individuals to Christ all around the world. Only in eternity will we know how many the two publications have brought to the cross of Jesus.

The same holds true with different translations of the Bible. Some cling to the belief that the King James is the only inspired version. I love the King James Version, but I personally prefer the New King James. Some favor the New International or Revised Standard Version better than other translations. Whatever version you prefer, take note that millions of Christians differ from you and believe they have the better translation.

The temperament that doesn't seem to care or say much about how we write, preach, teach, or what translation of God's Word we read from, though, is the peaceful phlegmatic. They're the easygoing ones who like to take a while before making decisions. Phlegmatics are thinkers and planners, "cool, detailed individuals who tend to limit themselves. They can do statistical, microscopic work that would drive others berserk" (*Why You Act the Way You Do,* p. 160).

While phlegmatics are strong introverts, it doesn't mean they are weak. The truth is, their calm and unexcited nature is a vital asset. They rarely, if ever, leap before they look. When witnessing to a phlegmatic, take it slowly. Usually they just listen and won't challenge what you present. But because they do not like changes, they sometimes will not accept what you have to say until they contemplate it for a while. Phlegmatics tend to clutter their lives with worry, fear, procrastination, and lack of motivation.

"Phlegmatics are nuts-and-bolts, quiet people who can be depended on if you keep their eyes on the goals. But you must set their goals. By nature they would accept 55 percent of their capability. They work best under pressure but balk at high pressure; so keep it gentle, reasonable, and encouraging" (*ibid.,* p. 186).

Like the sanguines, phlegmatics need plenty of approval. Although they may never defy you, don't be surprised if they ignore you. Because they are daydreamers they need constant reminders. Also they are natural *"rule worshipers."* It causes them to be satisfied with the way things are, so it isn't wise to change things too fast. God's peacemakers, they are great in board meetings, because they say very little, being usually quiet, gentle, gracious, and peaceful people. Probably they have the only temperament trait that causes them to act like a Christian before they actually become one.

Because phlegmatics do not like confrontations they sometimes will join the church on the shirttail of their spouse. Some may never really have a full conversion experience, but we cannot be the judge of that.

One of the phlegmatic's primary strengths is a love and sympathy for other people. But their greatest weakness is their lack of motivation. They wrote the book on procrastination and also have a strong tendency to quit a project shortly after starting it. As a result they seldom get involved in the Lord's work. And no one can be a more professional worrier than a phlegmatic.

Phlegmatic Strengths
1. Witty and hide emotions
2. Low-key and dependable
3. Most well-adjusted to life
4. Sympathetic

5. Calm, cool, and collected

6. Avoid conflicts at all cost

7. Efficient and neat

8. Excel under pressure

9. Have many friends

10. Good listeners

11. Enjoy watching people

12. Peaceful and pleasant

13. Rely heavily on data, analysis, and logic to make decisions

14. Outline the tradeoffs of their position and the options of others

15. Thoroughly examine and study people's needs and situations

16. Methodically and consistently follow procedures or policies

17. Like working with the tried and true

18. Like getting the most out of what already exists

Phlegmatic Weaknesses

1. Unenthusiastic and often shy

2. Indecisive and fearful

3. Can be quite stubborn

4. Not goal-oriented

5. Resist change

6. Can be lazy and careless

7. Too compromising

8. Not motivated easily

9. Indifferent

10. May confuse people with too many options, preventing action

11. May take too much time researching, making others feel uninterested

12. May not be flexible enough to provide concessions that would help solve a problem

13. May not appreciate new ideas and may not respond enthusiastically to change

14. May get too involved in data and fail to appreciate other people's lack of interest

How to influence and motivate the phlegmatic:

1. Be organized.

2. Show purpose.

3. Be detail-oriented.

4. Be systematic.

5. Be objective.

6. Always be fair and consistent.

Phlegmatics "make friends easily and are loved by everyone. However, they tend to procrastinate over almost everything, including Bible study and prayer" (*Ministry,* January 1997, p. 19).

How to be the most effective leader for a phlegmatic:

1. Present ideas as being as low-risk as possible.

2. Give opportunity to be analytical.

3. Exercise logic (employing facts and structure).

4. Try to tie new things to old ones.

"His work always bears the hallmark of neatness and efficiency. Although he is not a perfectionist, he does have exceptionally high standards of accuracy and precision" (*Why You Act the Way You Do,* p. 67).

How to be the best volunteer for phlegmatics:

1. Always move ahead slowly.

2. Always use logic.

3. Pay attention.

4. Be systematic.

5. Do your homework.

Characteristics of the most effective environment for phlegmatics:

1. Unemotional

2. Factual

3. Inquiring

4. Practical

Least effective environment for phlegmatics:

1. Constant rule changes

2. Highly emotional situations

3. Premature decisions

4. Ideas not taken seriously

Unlike the sanguines and cholerics, phlegmatics blossom on routines. They "avoid being in charge of anything." "Often the reason phlegmatics won't decide is they know the other person will do it his way anyway" (*Personality Plus*, pp. 185, 186).

Strengths phlegmatics will bring to the church:

1. Able to keep a cool head in the midst of crisis

2. Weigh pros and cons and can see tradeoffs in situations

3. Think before they act and will check the facts

4. Take things one step at a time to cover all bases

5. Make the most of what already exists before going to the new

6. Test to make sure things work

How those with the phlegmatic temperament help:

1. Offer practical and informative advice

2. Analyze problems thoroughly

3. Recognize the pros and cons of everything

To communicate with phlegmatic volunteers:

1. Focus on reason
2. Use facts and figures
3. Be organized

To communicate with phlegmatic leaders:

1. Progress slowly
2. Use logic
3. Be precise

Phlegmatics' views of others

Sanguines:

1. Too people-oriented
2. Not practical enough
3. Joke too much
4. Disregard rules
5. Too emotional

Cholerics:

1. Too impulsive
2. Possibly dangerous
3. Disregard costs
4. Too demanding, uncaring, and legalistic

Melancholies:

1. Too emotional
2. Not objective enough
3. Need to be more consistent
4. Need to lighten up and not take themselves so seriously
5. Too critical of others

Other phlegmatics:

1. Too precise
2. Too factual
3. Locked into only one set of data

Once the Holy Spirit fills phlegmatics, they will have a strong faith to trust God in anything. Because they are people-oriented, they make great teachers. Of the four temperaments, the phlegmatics are your best prayer warriors.

They need a little extra shove to accept things, but do so carefully. "You may need to push your phlegmatics gently out of the boat, much like a mother eagle pushes her young out of the nest. Just be there to lift them up if they begin to flounder. Offer spiritual resuscitation if they take in too much water" (*Ministry,* January 1997, p. 19).

Phlegmatics have an unexcited good humor that keeps them from being intensely involved in humdrum experiences. At times they seem to have a distinguished wit and a sense of timing in the art of comedy along with an active imagination.

Each of the temperaments faces the dilemma of being selfish, but the phlegmatic particularly struggles with the problem. They can be the most stubborn of the temperaments, making it extremely difficult to study with or witness to them. "They will almost never openly confront another person or refuse to do something, but they will somehow manage to sidestep the demand" (*Why You Act The Way You Do,* p. 81).

Phlegmatics will almost never argue with you while you study with them. If they do not see your point at first, they usually will sit quietly and look puzzled. At this your best bet is to leave the issue and come back to it later. The temperament must be studied with slowly, one day at a time, and shown true love and care.

"Character is power. The silent witness of a true, unselfish, godly life carries an almost irresistible influence. By revealing in our own life the character of Christ we cooperate with Him in the work of saving souls. It is only by revealing in our life His character that we can cooperate with Him. And the wider the sphere of our influence, the more good we may do. When those who profess to serve God follow Christ's example, practicing the principles of the law in their daily life; when every act bears witness that they love God supremely and their neighbor as themselves, then will the church have power to move the world" (*Christ's Object Lessons,* p. 340).

Conclusion

IN ORDER to receive God's help, man must realize his weakness and deficiency; he must apply his own mind to the great change to be wrought in himself; he must be aroused to earnest and persevering prayer and effort. Wrong habits and customs must be shaken off; and it is only by determined endeavor to correct these errors and to conform to right principles that the victory can be gained. Many never attain to the position that they might occupy, because they wait for God to do for them that which He has given them power to do for themselves. All who are fitted for usefulness must be trained by the severest mental and moral discipline, and God will assist them by uniting divine power with human effort" (*Patriarchs and Prophets,* p. 248).

I hope the simple, down-to-earth approaches to witnessing in this book have been helpful. Keep in mind that the temperament theory is not the final answer to witnessing. It is not a cure for everything, and like any good concept, it can be abused. We must consider more than just a person's temperament when witnessing. In the first place, we may make a wrong decision about what that temperament is, and second, we may forget the person while concentrating on their personality. If we start out on a wrong premise, we will end up with a wrong conclusion. But I believe this theory is the most helpful explanation as to why people do not always accept Christ when or how we would like them to. By keeping these simple principles in mind, you will find that those you are trying to bring to the cross will communicate with you better and you will bring more people to Christ. Good communication skills are vital for any successful witnessing program to work.

Sanguines, phlegmatics, cholerics, and melancholies will each approach Bible studies and the worship service differently. It doesn't do any good to debate with those who choose not to accept your witnessing. Remember, you can't lead others to Christ if you're at war with them. That is one reason it is so important to witness in such a way that you are not sparring with them, but are on the same side. Unless we as Christians demonstrate healthy traits in our own characters, our missionary endeavors will have no success in introducing Christ to the lost.

I cannot emphasize enough that only those who understand the gospel and know Christ as their personal Saviour will be able to witness to others effectively. And understanding the gospel does not come automatically. We cannot assume that just because we are church members and have been reared in the church, we fully understand the gospel. Daily we must go to the fountain of living water and drink of its pure elixir of life before we can share it with others. That is the only thing that will empower us to find true disciples for Christ. Not until we have satisfied our own thirst will we be ready to share that water with others. "He who drinks of the living water becomes a fountain of life. The receiver becomes a giver" (*The Ministry of Healing,* p. 102).

Understanding the strengths and weaknesses of the various human temperaments is a giant step toward knowing how to share your faith with those who have come thirsty and searching for the water that only Jesus can give. Consequently, if we attempt to share our faith without understanding how to offer it, our witnessing will be of no effect and will only damage the potential convert.

Because God has commissioned us to make disciples of those to whom we witness (Matt. 28:19, 20), our goal should be to learn all we can on how to share our faith effectively and be *properly trained.* "Many feel that they are fitted for a work *that they know scarcely anything about;* and if they start to labor in a self-important manner, they will fail to receive that knowledge which they must obtain in the school of Christ. These will be doomed to struggle with many difficulties, for which they are wholly unprepared. They will ever lack experience and wisdom until they learn their great inefficiency.

"Very much has been lost to the cause by the defective labors of men who possess ability, but who have *not had proper training.* They have engaged in a work which they knew not how to manage, and as the result have accomplished but little. They have not done a tithe of what they could have done had they received the right discipline at the start. They seized upon a few ideas, managed to get a runway of a few discourses, and here their progress ended. They felt competent to be teachers, when they had scarcely mastered their *abc* in the knowledge of the truth. They have been stumbling along ever since, not doing justice to themselves or to the work. They do not seem to have sufficient interest to arouse their dormant energies, or to tax their powers to become efficient workers. They have not taken pains to form thorough and well-devised plans, and their work shows deficiency in every part" (*Gospel Workers,* p. 78; italics supplied).

I've recently discovered that many huge businesses base their success on the temperament theory. Theodore Levitt wrote an article entitled "The Managerial Merry-go-round," in which he points out that "people have different cognitive styles—that is, ways of gathering and evaluating information. Some are systematic thinkers, others intuitive, some are receptive thinkers and others perceptive thinkers. These styles seem to be inherent and are fairly fixed by the time people reach maturity. What is even more instructive is that the research found that these styles greatly affect the way people perform the jobs they choose, and even determine the industries they enter" (*Why You Act the Way You Do,* p. 170). If the business world recognizes that it is worthwhile to train their people at every level, shouldn't we?

God doesn't ask us all to hit a home run every time we stand up to bat, but He does request that we be faithful in all we do. Because God holds the keys to our future, we have nothing to worry about in anything that we do for Him. It's one thing to be concerned about our future, but quite another to worry about it. When we commit our life to God, then our future will take care of itself.

Our relationship with Jesus today is the essence of our Christian service tomorrow (1 Cor. 15:10; Phil. 2:13). I have to keep reminding myself of the fact that Jesus has given us many Bible texts promising to be with us (Matt. 28:20; Acts 4:31; 18:10; 23:11; 27:23). We can be effective servants only as we learn to trust Him fully (John 15:5). When the

Word becomes part of our life (Ps. 119:11; John 1:1, 9, 12, 13), service to Him becomes a pleasure. Any apparent failure on our part will evaporate along with any concerns we might have about sharing our faith (Phil. 4:13, 19). Daily we must ask God to help us in developing our capacity to love sinners and have a passionate burden to bring them to Christ (Rom. 1:9; Col. 4:12; 1 Thess. 3:10). And as He enables us to love and accept them regardless of their physical appearance, behavior, and belief, we will find it easier getting acquainted and accepting their temperaments as well. Ellen White points out that "we must not live for self, blending into the darkness of the world; but kept from its evil we must give our lives into an active, earnest service, as faithful soldiers for the Captain of our salvation. This will sanctify the soul. *While we seek the salvation and benefit of others,* we shall be workers together with God, *learning His methods and partaking of His power.* . . . The real manifestation of Christ dwelling in your heart will be recognized by a well-ordered life and conversation. Your life will shine with the graces of the Spirit; meekness, kindness, tender compassion, the love of Jesus, and genuine lowliness of heart, will characterize your daily walk" (*Signs of the Times,* Dec. 15, 1887; italics supplied).

Remember, no one temperament is better than another. We are all different and have inherited the temperament that makes us the way we are. As individuals we act differently, respond differently, and perceive things differently. Each temperament fits the way God designed. That is why I pray that as doctors and psychologists continue to research the human mind, trying to understand our natural traits, work habits, and social habits, we will find a continuing use of the four-temperament theory in witnessing. We can take their research and use it to the glory of God. But always keep in mind that "we need to pray most earnestly and believe most trustingly, that the merits of Jesus Christ will suffice to bring grace and strength and determination to *enable us to overcome every defect.* O pray that 'the eyes of your understanding are being enlightened.' . . . *How many who are retaining their own ways and habits and practices, think that they cannot overcome, and so make no determined effort. They accept the old natural hereditary tendencies, and cherish them, as though they were the most precious jewels.* If they are reproved or counseled, they manifest a murmuring spirit, and retaliate upon the one who watches for their souls as one who must give an account. Others show disrespect to the one who points out to them the fact that they are misrepresenting the Saviour by *cherishing un-Christlike traits of character*. These poor souls need to be converted" (*Youth's Instructor,* Aug. 24, 1893; italics supplied).

Now that you have read this book and have a better understanding of the basic theory, you will have a jump on how to witness better for Christ. And if you have fully turned your life over to the Holy Spirit, you will have a better handle on overcoming your own weaknesses and maximizing your potential.

"The Christian will not be unyielding and dictatorial, but will consider himself a learner in Christ's school. He will not be of that class who are fond of lecturing others, sermonizing, condemning, criticizing, but will become meek and lowly in heart, representing Jesus, the Light of the world" (*Signs of the Times,* Dec. 15, 1887).